Quit Smoking

Other books by Curtis W. Casewit

Graphology Handbook
Freelance Writing: Advice from the Pros
Strategies to get the Job You Want

Quit Smoking

Para Research
Rockport
Massachusetts

Quit Smoking
by Curtis W. Casewit

Copyright © 1983 Curtis W. Casewit

Library of Congress Catalog Card Number: 83-060346
International Standard Book Number: 0-914918-44-3

Typeset in 10 pt. Paladium on Compugraphic MCS/8400
Printed by Alpine Press, Inc.
on 55-pound Surtone II Antique
Edited by Marah Ren and Shaun Levesque
Graphics by Robert Killam
Typeset by Jean King

Published by Para Research, Inc.
Whistlestop Mall
Rockport, Massachusetts 01966

Manufactured in the United States of America

First Printing, February 1983, 8,000 copies

Contents

Introduction

by
Sidney L. Werkman, M.D.
Professor of Psychiatry
University of Colorado Health Sciences Center
Denver, Colorado

Most books simply entertain or instruct. Rarely, a book comes along that can save lives. This is one of those books. It is filled with good news and good suggestions for cigarette smokers who want to live.

What better reasons for discontinuing cigarette smoking than these: More than 100,000 Americans die of lung cancer yearly—98 percent of them smoke cigarettes. The one-pack-a-day smoker runs about twice the risk of heart attack as the nonsmoker. The two-pack-a-day smoker has about three times the risk of a nonsmoker.

The good news is that heart disease rates are half as high among former smokers as among those who continue to smoke, and after five to ten years of not smoking, former smokers have almost identical life expectancies as those who have never smoked at all. Cessation of smoking does have a beneficial effect and even the damage caused by years of smoking appears largely to be reversible.

Quit Smoking offers an excellent overview of the problems of smoking and shows a promise, the light at the end of the tunnel, for smokers interested in kicking their habit. It is also an exhaustive, definitive text on all aspects of smoking. Never have I seen such a fine discussion of the whole realm of smoking concerns—history, psychology, physiology, treatment techniques and benefits.

Most of us are puzzled that a sophisticated technological society that has rid the country of typhoid fever, malaria and smallpox, tolerates the large number of deaths due to smoking. Curtis Casewit tells us why cigarette advertising and marketing are on the increase rather than the wane. Overall cigarette advertising expenditures have doubled in the last decade, to $1.2 billion dollars. You would think that our society would be more sensible, but as Mr. Casewit so deftly points out, the cigarette lobby has tremendous influence in the Congress today.

The dangers are not only for those hooked on smoking, but also for non-smokers who passively inhale smoke in restaurants, airplanes, public meeting places. Is it not time that efforts be made to protect the lungs and lives of innocent bystanders?

The issues are somewhat similar to those showing the relationship between television violence and the prevalence of violence in our society. Viewers become programmed to carry out the behaviors shown on television and in enticing advertisements. *Quit Smoking* asks how a society can allow itself to be bombarded with harmful media material. It is a call to arms for all citizens to remain healthy.

The answer is to stop smoking, but that is, as in so many things, easier said than done. In *Quit Smoking* we have an important statement of the whole variety of stop smoking programs. As Mr. Casewit points out "will power" is not the only way to success. A whole range of useful programs have been developed including group support, group therapy, biofeedback, acupuncture, meditation and hypnosis, guided imagery, behavior modification. This book will be useful for smokers who want to save their lives, for teachers and even for researchers in the field of habit pattern disturbances.

We must recognize that stop smoking programs (like weight reduction programs), though extremely successful in the short run, have a high relapse rate. Approximately 85 percent of smokers or obese people who lose a significant amount of weight will have started smoking and/or gained back all their weight within one year. Further research and clinical efforts need to be directed in two areas—to discover the factors that allow that 25 percent to give up smoking forever, and what new techniques need to be developed for the unfortunate 75 percent who relapse. This book, however, allows the reader to choose the cessation method that he or she thinks will work best.

Quit Smoking covers all the bases of the smoking baseball field—the programs, the therapies, the statistics, the problem itself. And, as a writer can describe best a problem that he has known personally, Curtis Casewit in a most charming way describes his own cigarette addiction and his successful cure of that habit. And he has not relapsed in 10 years!

He shows what an insidious problem marketing and consumer advertising for smoking has become. From an earlier emphasis on acceptability and sexual attractiveness of smokers, advertising has now invaded one of the most pristine areas of life, adventure travel. An adventurer or mountaineer is shown, cigarette in mouth, in glossy full-page advertisements. Just as we must stamp out the equation that makes violence attractive on television, we must stamp out the one that suggests that a person becomes more sexually attractive, strong, environmentally sophisticated if he or she smokes. And, as an afterthought, we might note how much cigarette advertisements have moved to attract women who have historically had lower lung cancer and cardiovascular disease rates. Instead of exulting in those figures, our society condones insidious advertising campaigns specifically directed toward women.

Quit Smoking tells it like it is, tells it all and tells what to do about it. Smokers need it, families of smokers need it and non-smokers need it. The value of a compendium like this is immense, and my hat is off to its author.

Preface

Ever since I gave up smoking, I have been fascinated—almost obsessed—with the topic. How do people get started with cigarettes? What do they really get out of smoking? And what, exactly, are the effects of the nicotine? I was haunted by the fact of psychological addiction, by the "habit" of smoking, and of course, by the health consequences.

It takes a former chain smoker to know a smoker.

I started with some exotic brands: deep puffs of French Gitanes and Gauloises during World War II; "Players" in the British Army; and biting, raw-tasting "Rothändle" in post-war Germany. Back home in the U.S., I switched to the potent Pall Malls, which are still in business and are high in tars, nicotine content and carbon monoxide.

Like many addicts, I fought a long battle until I finally managed to quit.

That glorious moment—freedom from cigarettes!—occurred more than a decade ago. I have not smoked since.

When I began to research this book, I decided that I would dig deeply and accumulate facts, figures, case histories, personalities, addresses. Instead of opting for the "instant" paperback, which is not uncommon these days, I would concentrate on creating a "catalogue," a complete stop smoking book.

Through the years, I spoke with experts in the field and interviewed physicians, psychiatrists, psychologists, government researchers, statisticians and assorted quitters of both sexes and of all ages. I collected boxes of interview notes. More: I kept abreast of new developments, including some ripoffs. I talked to the M.D.s who run stop-smoking clinics and to the new crop of Behavioral Scientists who try to cope with ending the public's self-abuse.

Acupuncture, hypnosis, fasting, aversion techniques, meditation, biofeedback all seemed worth examining. This meant that I would break new ground because little has been written about the new quitting methods.

Indeed, it is startling that up to now, no author took an in-depth look at cigarette smoking and at the many cessation programs available. True, there have always been books about one method or another; no one researcher, though, has managed to accumulate *all* the facts.

This book offers another "first": It examines the battles fought by the Tobacco Lobby against the U.S. Surgeon General and, among others, against the valiant American Cancer Society. Even the nonsmoker is bound to be entertained by the tug-of-war between the powerful cigarette industry and the U.S. government, and by an inside analysis of how tobacco advertising attempts to manipulate us. This advertising works, too, judging by the whopping U.S. sale figures—620 billion cigarettes a year.

As a result, cigarette smoking has become the greatest environmental cause of death in America. It claims almost 400,000 lives a year and leads to various afflictions for a horrendous number of people. Some of the newly discovered medical consequences that can befall smokers are outlined in Chapter 4. The health hazard has been one major factor for the army of quitters that includes more than 110,000 U.S. doctors. According to a national survey, six out of ten smokers have seriously tried to stop.

However, it also seemed to me that the North American story was not enough. I therefore traveled to a number of European countries for more information. What stop-smoking products are available in France? How does the German government deal with cigarettes? And how successful are the Swedes with their campaigns for a "smokeless year 2000"? An honest, up-to-date report about the Swedish situation can be found in Chapter 14.

This book deals exclusively with cigarettes from all angles; I've left the pleasures and perils of the pipe, the cigar and marijuana to other medical journalists.

In the many years of researching and writing, I was assisted by a great number of individuals and organizations.

I would like to acknowledge the major contributions of Washington's well-staffed "Office on Smoking and Health" (formerly the "National Clearinghouse for Smoking and Health"), the American Cancer Society, the World Health Organization in Geneva; Dr. Tommy Kofoed, Five Day Plan; Dr. Arthur Ulene, National Broadcasting Company; Dr. Ernest Wynder, American Health Foundation; John W. Nawratil, Editor, *American Journal of Acupuncture*; Dr. Sidney Werkman, Professor of Psychiatry, University of Colorado School of Medicine; Dr. Robert I. Levy, National Heart, Lung and Blood Institute; Dr. Bryan Brook and Dr. A. B. Craig, psychologists; Mary Anne Wallendjack, the Sutphen Seminars; Dr. Paul Hansen and Gerald Ferrone, Continental Health Enhancement Centers; Dr. Terrence Hansen, St. Helena Hospital; and Dr. Johannes Brengelmann of the Max Planck Psychiatric Institute, Munich, West Germany.

I also want to thank the Swedish National Smoking and Health Association, the American Lung Association, the U.S. Public Health Service, the American Heart Association, Action on Smoking and Health (ASH), the

Xerox Health Management Program, the Mercy Medical Center and SmokEnders for various courtesies. Lastly, Doug Hall, Frank Molinski and Shaun Levesque all deserve praise for their backing of this project. Additional research by Norman Ford, June Julian and Niccolo Casewit enriched this book.

I hope it proves helpful to a large readership.

1

The History of Cigarettes and Tobacco

A fifth century bas-relief found in the Palenque ruins of Southern Mexico is one of the oldest representations of a smoker that has been found anywhere in the world. It shows a Mayan shaman wearing a tobacco leaf crown as he puffs away on a large cigar.

The Warao Indians of Venezuela used tobacco for magic and in their prayer rituals. The Aztecs, too, smoked primitive cigarettes. They put tobacco in a hollow reed or tube. The natives of Mexico, Central America and South America crushed tobacco leaves and rolled these shreds in vegetable wrappers, such as corn-husks, to create makeshift cigars.

Much of this strenuous tobacco smoking was related to a tobacco religion. The Plains Indians of North America had the most elaborate ceremonies. The purification ritual and the Sun Dance involved serious tobacco consumption. The sacred truce area during the deadliest of Indian wars was in Pipestone, Minnesota, the area to which many tribes annually traveled in order to mine the red rock, from which they carved the bowls of their peace pipes. The favorite smoking mixture for many of the U.S. tribes in the north and Canada was then "Kinnikinnik," a blend of sumac leaves, dogwood bark and tobacco. Moreover, tobacco was also snuffed, chewed and eaten.

When Christopher Columbus arrived in the New World in 1492, he saw natives using tobacco in ways we do today—for smoking and masticating and as snuff. Columbus saw men on the island of Cuba sucking on leaves. The plant was called "Caoba."

Tobacco was introduced to Europe in 1559, probably by Francisco Hernandez de Toledo who was the physician to Philip II of Spain. The Spaniards, incidentally, were the first Europeans to cultivate the plant. In 1560, it was brought to the French court by Jean Nicot de Villemain, the French ambassador to Lisbon. We owe Nicot the botanical term, "Nicotiana" and also the word nicotine. Sailors showed up with tobacco in England around 1565, and in 1586, Sir Francis Drake learned about it from the "Red Indians" of Virginia. By 1592, Sir Walter Raleigh, a colorful favorite in Queen Elizabeth's court, popularized it in England.

During the sixteenth century tobacco leaves were thought to have great medicinal value by physicians. Nicot gave snuff to Catherine de Medici and her court to cure migraines. Also it was thought to cure colds, fever and to protect people from the plague.

However, at the same time, tobacco use was strongly opposed. Perhaps the most famous warning came from James I of England in 1604. He was one of history's most famous tobacco phobiacs. His famous "A Counter Blaste to Tobacco" describes his negative view of smoking: "Herein is not only a great vanity but a great contempt of God's good gifts, that the sweetness of man's breath should be willfully corrupted by this stinking smoke...a custom loathesome to the eye, hateful to the nose, harmful to the brain, dangerous to the lungs."

The Ottoman Emperor, Amurat IV, actually sentenced smokers to death. One czar resorted to whippings and noseslittings of smokers, and during the sixteenth century the Shah Sifi had smokers impaled.

At that time in Europe, poor man's smokes were known as "Papeletes" or "Cigarellos." It was not until late in the eighteenth century that smoking acquired respectability and the practice spread to Italy and Portugal. From there the small cigars were carried by Portuguese traders to Russia. The French and British troops fighting each other on Spanish soil in the Napoleonic campaign of 1814 became familiar with the light smokes as well as with cigars. It was in France that they acquired the name of cigarettes.

America's commercial involvement with tobacco began more than 350 years ago when a young Englishman named John Rolfe was said to have acquired seeds from the Spanish colonies of Trinidad and Caracus. According to the U.S. Tobacco Institute, early settlers found the leaves growing near the settlement named for England's James I and they described it as "poore and weake, and of a byting tast."

In 1612, just two years after his arrival in Jamestown, one settler planted the first crop of "Nicotiana tabacum," the milder Spanish leaf introduced earlier in Europe. In the words of one prominent tobacco historian, "never was a marriage of soil and seed more fruitful."

The harvest was unlike tobacco as we know it today. Although far superior in quality to the native leaf, the heavy, strong product would most closely resemble the coarsest, darkest type of chewing tobacco now sold.

As more colonists reached the New World, cultivation of tobacco spread. At one time or another, every colony along the Atlantic seaboard grew the leaf. However, Virginia and Maryland remained the center of this agriculture.

The tobacco economy of colonial times provided the impetus for settlers to move north, south and west in search of virgin lands. With fertilization and crop rotation techniques unknown, farmers tended to use the soil until it was exhausted, then move on to new land and plant anew.

What is now Delaware was the first North American colony founded expressly to produce export tobacco. Although that project failed because of Indian hostility, George Calver, the first Lord Baltimore, asked for and received a grant for land along the Chesapeake Bay where he could "do the King and Country more service" by planting more tobacco. His Maryland colony was established in 1634.

By the 1650s planters were beginning to amass the large, self-sustaining plantations that would encourage the widespread use of Negro slavery. Virginians moved into the Albemarle area of Carolina in search of better soil for tobacco; other settlers extended the borders of the Old Dominion into the Piedmont and Blue Ridge districts. As the eighteenth century came to a close, restless planters were crossing into what is now Tennessee and Kentucky, Ohio and farther west, to make permanent settlements in new lands where they could grow tobacco.

The First Problems

Tobacco use was first associated with the possible development of cancer as early as the late seventeenth century. One medical historian, Dr. John Hill, should be credited with the first report documenting an association between tobacco use and cancer for his work, "Cautions Against the Immoderate Use of Snuff." Hill reported on two case histories and observed that "snuff is able to produce . . . swellings and excrescences" in the nose, and he believed these to be cancerous.

It was not until the 1920s and 1930s that investigators began to examine scientifically the possible association of smoking and cancer. In 1928, two American physicians found an association between heavy smoking and cancer in general.

According to a U.S. government source, the first major developments in the modern history of investigation of the effects of smoking on health occurred in 1950 with the publication of four retrospective studies on smoking habits of lung cancer patients in the United States. Each of these early experts noted a consistent, statistically significant association betwen smoking and cancer of the lungs. Other investigators proceeded to further examine the relationship by initiating prospective studies in which large numbers of healthy persons were followed over time and the reasons for their deaths noted. Again, the investigators found a statistical correrlation between smoking and cancer.

A Warning From Great Britain

In late 1959 and early 1960, the American Cancer Society enrolled over one million men and women in a prospective study. Although this was not a representative sample of the United States population, all segments of the population were included except groups that the planners believed could not be traced easily. An initial questionnaire was administered that contained information on age, sex, race, education, place of residence, family history, past diseases, present physical complaints, occupational exposures and various habits. Information on smoking included the number of cigarettes smoked per day, inhalation, age started smoking and the brand of cigarettes used.

Nearly 93 percent of the survivors were successfully monitored for a twelve-year period. Early reports of this study examined lung cancer mortality in relationship to several parameters of smoke exposure, including duration of habit and age at onset, among others. Two recent reports have examined the effects of general air pollution, the type of cigarette smoked, and lung cancer mortality. Cancer mortality data for 483,000 white females and 358,000 white males for a four-year period were also reported.

The U.S. Veterans' study followed the mortality experience of 290,000 U.S. veterans who held government life insurance policies. Almost all policyholders were white males. The data for specific causes of death during a sixteen-year period were recently reported and the findings about the smoking/cancer connection were similar to those of earlier studies.

Cigarette advertising has been a major concern of the Federal Trade Commission since it began examining the first cigarette advertisements. The FTC's first actions prevented cigarette companies from making unsupported claims about the medical and other benefits of particular brands. In the period up to 1960, the Commission issued seven cease and desist orders prohibiting various false claims in cigarette advertising. Then the Commission shifted its attention to industry-wide regulation and announced Cigarette Advertising Guides. In 1960, the Commission began arguing with the leading cigarette manufacturers about getting rid of untrue "tar" and nicotine content facts in their advertising.

The U.S. Surgeon General Makes History

In 1964 the Advisory Committee to the Surgeon General of the U.S. Public Health Service published a comprehensive review of all available data. The Committee reported that "cigarette smoking is causally related to lung cancer in men; the magnitude of the effect of cigarette smoking far outweighs all other factors. Data for women, though less extensive, point in the same direction. The risk of developing lung cancer increases with the duration of smoking and the number of cigarettes smoked per day and is diminished by discontinuing smoking."

The Federal Trade Commission responded swiftly to the Surgeon General's report and took its first formal action in 1964 to require that cigarette manufacturers warn consumers of the health hazards of smoking. Given the "mounting evidence . . . of the very grave hazards to life and health involved in cigarette smoking," the Commission found that failure of the manufacturers to warn consumers of the danger was an unfair and deceptive practice that violated Section 5 of the Federal Trade Commission Act.

In 1965 Congress pre-empted the FTC action by enacting legislation that required all cigarette packages sold in the United States to include the statement: "Caution: Cigarette Smoking May Be Hazardous To Your Health." In addition, the Cigarette Act prohibited the FTC from requiring any other statement on the cigarette package or in cigarette advertisements. The Act also directed the Commission to submit an annual report to Congress on cigarette advertising.

Over the last seventeen years, thousands of scientific investigations have confirmed and provided additional evidence concerning the relationship between cigarette smoking and lung cancer. Smoking has been implicated as a cause of cancer of the larynx, oral cavity and esophagus, and associated with cancer of the urinary bladder, kidney and pancreas.

Then, in mid-1969, the FTC proposed a modified version of the 1964 Rule that would require all cigarette advertisements to carry the following message: "Warning: Cigarette Smoking is Dangerous to Health and May Cause Death From Cancer, Coronary Heart Disease, Chronic Bronchitis, Pulmonary Emphysema and other diseases." Congress, however, amended the message on cigarette packages to read: "Warning: The Surgeon General Has Determined that Cigarette Smoking is Dangerous to Your Health."

Moreover, since 1971 it has been illegal to advertise cigarettes on television or radio. Prior to this, the cigarette companies were heavy users of the air media; since then, they have become heavy users of newspapers, magazines and outdoor advertising. Advertising and promotion spending between 1970 and 1978 more than doubled, from $361 to $874 million. Cigarettes are believed to account for 32 percent of all outdoor advertising and 9 percent of all consumer magazine advertising.

Then in 1982 the Surgeon General's report described more grim facts about the bad health effects of cigarettes. The content of this report is the work of numerous scientists as well as scientific experts outside the U.S. government. Individual manuscripts were reviewed by experts, and the entire report was reviewed by a panel of twelve distinguished scientists. Many of these scientists are, or have been, directly involved in research on the health effects of smoking.

Provisional mortality data for a typical year indicated that cancer was responsible for approximately 412,000 deaths in the United States. It is estimated that in 1982 there will be 430,000 deaths due to cancer, 233,000 among men and 197,000 among women. Various investigators have suggested that 22 to 38 percent of these deaths can be attributed to smoking, and therefore were potentially "avoidable" if the subjects had not been smokers. Also, overall cancer mortality rates among smokers are dose-related as measured by the number of cigarettes smoked per day. Heavy smokers (over one pack per day) have more than three times the overall cancer death rate of nonsmokers. With increasing duration of smoking cessation, overall cancer death rates decline, approaching the death rate of nonsmokers.

The report showed how smoking also triggers malignancies of the mouth, esophagus and larynx, in addition to lung cancer, which is now the nation's leading killer. Also, smoking is a "contributory factor" in cancers of the pancreas, bladder and kidney. Further, smokers are prone to an "excess mortality" from cancers of the stomach and cervix. Some surveys have suggested that an increased risk of lung cancer may be probable for nonsmokers who inhale other people's smoke. "Prudence indicates that nonsmokers avoid exposure to secondhand tobacco smoke to the extent possible." Also, the Surgeon General maintained that smoking is "the most important public health issue of our time."

Death rates by number of cigarettes smoked daily				
	Number of cigarettes smoked daily			
Age	1-9	10-19	20-39	40+
Males				
45-54	741	910	970	1,109
55-64	1,815	2,280	2,437	2,680
65-74	4,683	5,145	5,325	5,635
Females				
45-54	288	368	464	592
55-64	682	904	1,010	1
65-74	2,055	2,238	2,862	1

Source: U.S. Government Printing Office

ASH

ASH, Action on Smoking and Health, a national nonprofit organization, became concerned with the problems of smoking and nonsmokers' rights. The group was particularly taken with the 1982 Surgeon General's conclusion, reached by an impartial and expert panel, that tobacco smoke may cause cancer in nonsmokers. The group reported that there are two major studies that show a statistically significant correlation between involuntary smoking and lung cancer risk in the nonsmoking wives of husbands who smoked. One showed a strikingly higher incidence of lung cancer among Greek women who had been or still were married to smokers. Compared with a control group, women who had been married to smokers increased their risk of lung cancer by 80 percent; women who were at the time married to light smokers had a 140 percent higher chance of getting lung cancer; and women married to heavy smokers had increased their lung cancer risk by 240 percent.

The Surgeon General's panel of experts studied the many constituents of tobacco smoke and noted that some of these are known carcinogens. Their report showed that these toxins are often present in far greater amounts in the sidestream smoke to which nonsmokers are exposed than in the mainstream smoke that goes directly into the smokers' lungs.

The conclusions were that "involuntary smoking may pose a carcinogenic risk to the nonsmoker"; that it poses "a serious public health concern because of the large numbers of nonsmokers in the population who are potentially exposed."

The Trend Against Cigarette Smoking

Other antismoking groups soon helped promote nonsmokers' rights by lobbying for antismoking legislations. Many groups created local chapters throughout the U.S. In addition to ASH, GASP (Group Against Smokers' Pollution), ANSR (Association for Nonsmokers' Rights), The National Organization of Nonsmokers and the National Interagency Council on Smoking and Health all helped the cause. Many of these organizations worked together to draft a document called the "Bill of Rights for Nonsmokers." It maintains that nonsmokers have certain rights: "The right to breathe clean air . . . free from harmful and irritating tobacco smoke. This right supercedes the right to smoke when the two conflict."

By 1982 many states across the nation had responded to the nonsmokers by passing legislation that restricted polluting public areas such as elevators, libraries, stores, hospitals and restaurants. Hypersensitive people, especially those with allergies, emphysema, heart disease, bronchitis and other chronic diseases were pleading for relief against the assault.

The Civil Aeronautics Board ruled that all passenger aircraft must designate nonsmoking areas in each class of service. In response to complaints from nonsmoking passengers and a government study showing that 60 percent of the abstaining passengers were bothered by cigarette fumes, airline companies were asked to carefully segregate passengers who smoke from those who do not.

Employers soon took steps to accommodate nonsmoking employees and to discourage smoking among their personnel. For example, some companies have designated nonsmoking and smoking work areas for their employees, and offer a cash bonus for quitting. They maintain that the increased productivity justifies the expense. In addition, some corporations forbid smoking on the job and encourage their employees to become anti-smoking activists. So not only have smokers been discriminated against in renting the apartment of their choice, or relegated to the rear of airplanes, or seated in the drafty section of restaurants, they are now being discriminated against in getting a job.

Much has been recently done by health organizations and community groups to educate smokers about the hazards of cigarettes and to provide encouragement to smokers in their fight to stop the habit. As part of its five-year action program, called Target Five, the American Cancer Society has formed a National Commission on Smoking and Public Policy. The twenty-five-member Commission is conducting public forums on smoking in major cities around the country, and its findings and recommendations will be used in future public education, information, legislative and regulatory campaigns. In 1981, when the American Cancer Society sponsored their fifth "Great American Smokeout," an estimated 18 million people pledged to survive twenty-four hours without a smoke. The American Cancer Society declares that most smokers want to quit.

2

The Psychology and Physiology of Smoking

Coffee break at a Manhattan office. There are five women in the bright room. Paper cup in hand, the supervisor reaches for her pack of cigarettes. Pulls one out, taps it lightly against the desk. Lights up. You see her take a deep breath, sending smoke through her well-shaped nostrils. Soon, two of the secretaries strike matches and begin the smoking ritual. Conversation flows easily now.

It is a pleasant, sociable moment. You light up, too. You like filter cigarettes. They are low in tars and have less than a milligram of nicotine. The aroma is satisfying. For some people, smoking has become almost a Pavlovian reflex; they seldom indulge alone. And it is true: the tobacco goes well with coffee and with your drink at night.

If you've ever smoked, you've experienced these companionable moments, this taking a break from life while in the community of others. I remember a summer night long ago in Wyoming. There were a dozen writers sitting around a remote Jackson Hole campfire. Some of us smoked; the stars stood out sharply above. A full moon shone down on us. It was a time for good company—and for cigarettes.

The motion pictures of the forties and fifties often showed us the great stars of the screen smoking. We now see fewer such screen gestures. Blame the Surgeon General who—for decades—gave the cigarette a black eye. (Ironically, Humphrey Bogart died of throat cancer while Gary Cooper eventually suffered from another carcinoma.)

Life has always been hard for a large portion of the population. Historically, tobacco brought pleasurable relief, offering a respite from work or despair. "Sublime tobacco!" Byron cried out in one of his poems. "When tipp'd with amber, rich and ripe—" And as far back as 1605, an English sea captain penned his doggerel,

> Tobacco, tobacco
> Sing sweetly for tobacco,
> Tobacco is like love, oh love it;
> For you see I have proved it.

Why People Smoke

The solace gained from smoking becomes evident when you see people behind the Iron Curtain. On a recent trip to Romania, for instance, I noticed that nearly everyone was puffing away. It seemed one of the local populace's scant pleasures; the people smoked even in the famous Romanian health clinics. Likewise, one cannot fault the unlucky Poles for reaching out to tobacco, despite price hikes. The smoke is a brief escape from a dull or menial job.

To be sure, cigarettes make a momentary dent in boredom. The truck driver on the endless Texas superhighway often indulges. Or observe a factory worker in Cincinnati or Century City; day after day, hour after hour, assembling the same tiny electronic parts. The monotony of the job is made more tolerable through periodic nicotine fixes.

People shuffle their packs of Camels or Kents as they stand in a seemingly endless postal line, waiting to buy Christmas stamps. The people in line smoke because it makes time seem to go faster and also because they are irritated with the time they have to waste in line. The hand-cradling of the cigarette box, the tapping of a filter against a hard surface are all good routine-breakers.

Naturally, among some groups of North Americans and Europeans— especially young women—cigarette smoking is a symbol of liberation. Once forbidden or looked upon with disfavor, smoking is now an option for women.

They can smoke now. And they do. Humorist Fran Lebowitz said it well enough: "Smoking is, if not my life, then at least my hobby. I love to smoke. Smoking is fun. Smoking is cool. Smoking is, as far as I am concerned, the entire point of being an adult. It makes growing up genuinely worthwhile. I am quite well aware of the hazards of smoking. Smoking is not a healthful pastime, it is true. Smoking is indeed no bracing dip in the ocean, no strenuous series of calisthenics, no two laps around the reservoir. On the other hand, smoking has to its advantage the fact that it is a quiet pursuit. Smoking is, in effect, a dignified sport."

Women account for the greatest number of new recruits to the nicotine vineyards. And at the same time, health authorities are alarmed by the dramatic figure of some 1.5 million American teenagers who start smoking each year. Not all of these youths will develop the habit. Most of them, so the experts tell us, take their first puff because of peer pressure.

Others frankly admit that they at first smoked as little kids "to show off." Some youngsters, at ages ten or eleven, want to do the forbidden thing; the secrecy adds to the excitement, of course. At the same time, particularly in the early teens, the reasons for smoking may be rejection of authority, acting "more grown up," curiosity or even a search for self-fulfillment. In time, young people can become hooked if they keep at it.

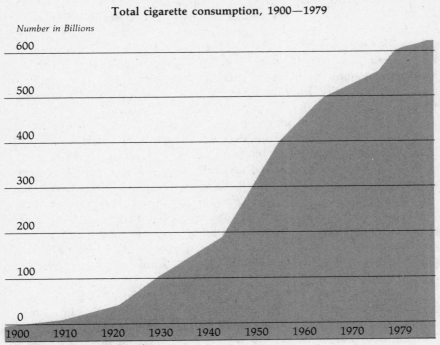

Total cigarette consumption, 1900—1979

Number in Billions

U.S.Department of Agriculture.

According to an American Cancer Society study, children are also enormously influenced by their parents; if their elders drink too much alcohol, the offspring may become alcoholics. If parents smoke, immature children often imitate them. (A detailed account of the situation and some remedies can be found in *The Stop Smoking Book for Teens*. See Bibliography.)

The Cigarette as a Stress Fighter

According to many respected researchers, a great number of adults, approximately 30 percent, also reach for a cigarette as a psychological coping mechanism against stress. Some people believe that they handle life's true emergencies better with a cigarette. Consider the extreme case of the prisoner condemned to death. The prisoner asks for—and receives—one last tobacco "treat" before being executed.

Closer to home, there are plenty of alarming situations. For instance: You learn one morning that your job is no longer secure; you (with a family to support) may be laid off. With such news, why shouldn't you dig into your pockets for a smoke? An older woman, who has long quit the habit, suddenly learns that her husband has decamped with a young girl. For good. Facing such a trauma, the ex-user rushes to her friendly drugstore for her tobacco-tranquilizer. Dr. James R. Craig, a psychologist, explains: "An individual faces many unpleasant moments in his or her life. The smoke becomes a form of stress management, an escape from stress. Unfortunately, this relief is only temporary and can become addictive...." Dr. Craig has known the high-powered "Type A" personalities who seem to cope with their high-pressure jobs in the stock market or in commerce thanks only to cigarettes. Naturally, you don't need to be a Type A person to appreciate stress.

Our working day is full of tensions. The telephone operator keeps you waiting; the plumber, despite promises, doesn't show up; a date—or mate—is heading for trouble; the bank informs us of an unexpected, perhaps unjust, overdraft. Minor stresses all, and all good reasons for the habituated to open another pack. The cigarette thus becomes a tranquilizer, a sedative.

In other cases—I recall my long nocturnal stints at the typewriter twenty years ago—we use tobacco as a pick-me-up. "Oh, cigarettes give me a lift," an office worker told me last week, adding, "I get so tired I couldn't exist without my smokes." In a series of interviews, Dr. Daniel Horn received similar answers. "I smoke to perk myself up." "I smoke to give myself a lift." "I smoke to keep myself from slowing down."

Researchers have discovered still other reasons. One group of psychiatrists claims that the habit is a regression to our infancy; the cigarette is something to suck on, i.e., smokers are really babies sucking at bottles. The oral satisfaction makes sense. An even more far-fetched theory has to do with pyromania, the desire to set fires; while this rare breed puffs away, they are actually stifling their arson drives.

According to Dr. Horn, about 10 percent of the cigarette addicts actually get nothing from it all. Dr. Horn refers to people who light one with another one barely touched, still smoldering in an ashtray. "The habitual smoker does so automatically," writes Dr. Horn. "He may smoke a cigarette without realizing it or even wanting it. There is very little emotional component to his smoking activity and minimal amount of awareness."

To be sure, for some people, the stimulation often comes first. They are addicted to the nicotine kick.

Test 1
Do You Want to Change Your Smoking Habits?

For each statement, circle the number that most accurately indicates how you feel. For example, if you completely agree with the statement, circle 4, if you agree somewhat, circle 3, etc.
Important: Answer every question.

	completely agree	somewhat agree	somewhat disagree	completely disagree
A. Cigarette smoking might give me a serious illness.	4	3	2	1
B. My cigarette smoking sets a bad example for others.	4	3	2	1
C. I find cigarette smoking to be a messy kind of habit.	4	3	2	1
D. Controlling my cigarette smoking is a challenge to me.	4	3	2	1
E. Smoking causes shortness of breath.	4	3	2	1
F. If I quit smoking cigarettes it might influence others to stop.	4	3	2	1
G. Cigarettes cause damage to clothing and other personal property.	4	3	2	1
H. Quitting smoking would show that I have willpower.	4	3	2	1
I. My cigarette smoking will have a harmful effect on my health.	4	3	2	1
J. My cigarette smoking influences others close to me to take up or continue smoking.	4	3	2	1
K. If I quit smoking, my sense of taste or smell would improve.	4	3	2	1
L. I do not like the idea of feeling dependent on smoking.	4	3	2	1

HOW TO SCORE:
1. Enter the numbers you have circled to the Test 1 questions in the spaces below, putting the number you have circled to Question A over line A, to Question B over line B, etc.
2. Total the 3 scores across on each line to get your totals. For example, the sum of your scores over lines A, E, and I gives you your score on *Health*—lines B, F, and J give the score on *Example*, etc.

Totals

____ + ____ + ____ = ____ Health
  A   E   I

____ + ____ + ____ = ____ Example
  B   F   J

____ + ____ + ____ = ____ Esthetics
  C   G   K

____ + ____ + ____ = ____ Mastery
  D   H   L

Scores can vary from 3 to 12. Any score 9 and above is *high*; any score 6 and below is *low*. From the Department of Health, Education and Welfare publication, *Smokers Self-Testing Kit*, 1975.

The Daily Nicotine Fix

Indeed, what happens physically when you smoke?

The nicotine acts with remarkable speed; it takes only an instant to be absorbed by your lungs and intestines. Within seconds, nicotine stimulates your brain and your autonomic nervous system. Your adrenal glands begin to work harder. Your heart rate and blood pressure go up. Respiration increases. In short, a little nicotine gets you high.

Long-time addicts know that the performance has to be repeated for more euphoria. As the nicotine level drops you begin to crave another cigarette. In the end, smoking acts as a depressant, much the same as the ten cups of coffee, or the pep pill. Dr. Paul A. Hansen, staff psychologist for the well-known Continental Health Evaluation Center near Boulder, Colorado, tells his patients that cigarettes give a "yoyo effect"; they lift you up, then let you down.

Physicians have accumulated a good many facts about chain-smoking. One report, for instance, catalogues the physiological consequences: "cold, clammy skin; increased acid production in the stomach and increased intestinal activity; changes in salivation, with an initial gland stimulation followed by a decrease..."

Luckily, after being metabolized by several organs including the liver, nicotine is finally expelled from your body, mostly via the kidneys.

How about the addictive process? Physicians have actually measured the physical steps at work within the chain smoker's body. In varying degrees, nicotine causes the liver to convert stored glycogen (animal starch) into glucose (sugar), which is released into the blood stream, causing a temporary lift. Excess insulin lowers the blood sugar level, causing fatigue, tension and the desire for another cigarette.

Few people seem to realize that nicotine happens to be a powerful poison; one drop on a rabbit's skin causes instant shock. If you limit yourself to only one pack a day, which the heavy smokers consider as moderate, you actually suck in 400 milligrams of the poison a week. One pathologist told me: "If 400 mg. were injected all at once, it would kill you quick as a bullet."

Maybe that's why a cigarette can be overpowering for the first-timer, especially a young person. I still remember a scene at the age of six or seven. A few kids had retreated into a mysterious forest at dusk. We found some small dry hollow flower stalks. Someone brought matches. We sucked in the hot smoke. We all began to cough, and to feel light-headed. There were ominous rumblings in my gut. Many years later, in the army, my first cigarette caused much nausea and a run to the latrines.

The trapped smoker quickly forgets such beginnings; instead, he or she begins to enjoy the sensations of renewed alertness and the new, temporary liveliness. The racing pulse seems exciting. Indeed, the user at once forgets—or perhaps doesn't realize—that pharmacologists label nicotine a *poison*.

It seems intriguing that the general public has little awareness about the genuine dangers of prolonged, heavy cigarette smoking. In an often-quoted Department of Health survey, for instance, a large segment of smokers claimed that they had never heard about the possibilities of future bronchitis, bladder cancer or circulation problems. And in a five-year study, the Federal Trade Commission reached the following conclusions:

24 percent of heavy smokers did not know smoking is dangerous;
40 percent did not know that smoking caused most cases of lung cancer;
60 percent did not know that smoking causes most cases of emphysema;
50 percent did not know that smoking causes many heart attacks;
50 percent of all teenagers did not know smoking is addictive;
41 percent of smokers did not know that smoking will shorten their expected lifespan.

Death rates by age started smoking
Rate per 100,000

| Age | Age started smoking | | | | |
	Under 14	15-19	20-24	25-29	30+
45-54	1,210	999	857	726	562
55-64	2,682	2,509	2,058	2,082	1,576
65-74	6,221	5,728	4,728	3,902	3,846

Source: U.S. Government Printing Office

Many nicotine freaks come up with convincing rationalizations for why they can't get off the weed. "I've this uncle, you see. He turned ninety this year. He smoked two packs a day all his life." This makes sense of course; some of us are blessed with such excellent genes that we can withstand a lifetime's insult to our lungs. There are people who say "smoking is my only vice, and everyone should be allowed one vice."

Others make assurances that they don't inhale, which is possible and positive. Or that they smoke only low-tar filter cigarettes (this can be a fallacy: the true addict increases the number of daily cigarettes, or inhales more deeply, to make up for the filters). You often hear that stopping is out of the question because the person would gain weight (this is a fallacy because only one-third of the quitters risk putting on some extra pounds).

So be it. The last word belongs to an unknown poet who wrote in a now defunct college paper, the *Penn State Froth*, almost seventy years ago:

Tobacco is a dirty weed. I like it.
It satisfies no normal need. I like it.
It makes you thin, it makes you lean,
It takes the hair right off your bean,
It's the worst darn stuff I've ever seen.
    I like it.

3

The Cigarette Industry

It's true that if you want to quit, the cigarette can become a formidable adversary. For some people, the smoke is a reward for hard work; for others, the not-to-be-taken-away pleasure after a gourmet dinner. According to Dr. Jerome Schwartz, a California expert, the most difficult times will be had by the "habit" smoker. "These are the people who get the crazies when they can't have a cigarette. They're addicts. They must rush out during a concert intermission . . ."

The world's celebrities are not immune, either. Somerset Maugham, the famous author, was known to smoke four packs a day. One night, to his discomfort, he was out of cigarettes in his French Riviera villa. As the story has it, the aging writer walked three kilometers for a new supply. At midnight, Sigmund Freud, ill with tobacco-caused malignant sores, continued to puff away despite the excruciating pain of having his inner jaw and palate "scraped" by his doctors at regular intervals. He was unable to quit and died in 1939, addicted to the end.

The habit can be so ingrained that Canadian hospital patients, their cancerous voice boxes already removed, continue to sneak cigarettes when the nurses are out of sight. Another example? A well-known movie star found that smoking caused her skin to develop career-killing wrinkles. She had complicated, costly plastic surgery. And then? She couldn't stop herself from smoking. And more wrinkles. "Once smoking really gets hold of you," a man told me, "there is little you can do against it. You're trapped. You can't even control the number of daily cigarettes. You're a junkie."

The demand for the intermittent fix can be so strong that it becomes irresistible. (An English tobacco company had good reasons for choosing "Craven A" cigarettes for a brand name.) To the true smoker, tobacco will be all-important. World War II German concentration camp data shows that even if there was no food, the users bartered their last crumbs for a cigarette. By 1945, when none could be bought, the nicotine hunger was still great enough for many Europeans to pick butts off the streets. Young women would beg for a smoke, or prostitute themselves for a carton of Pall Malls.

According to Dr. E.J. Beattie, Sloan Kettering, nicotine is "as physically addictive a drug as heroine or morphine." In the same sense, the National Institute of Drug Abuse has decided that *habitual* (not occasional) cigarette smoking must be classed as "physically and psychologically addictive behavior." And, heroin addicts admit that cigarettes are more difficult to give up. The one after-dinner cigarette doesn't propel you into being hooked, but the day-long *repetition* of smoking will. Dr. Michael Crichton once explained it best of all. "I know," he said, "the repeated desire to smoke was not in my reasoning mind. It had to be in my subconscious memory." And the seesaw of craving, with only a partial fulfillment, was well-described by Oscar Wilde who wrote: "A cigarette is the perfect type of the perfect pleasure. It is exquisite and it leaves one unsatisfied. What more can you want?"

Advertising Power

To be sure, the tobacco addiction is generated and later reinforced by powerful merchandising forces—America's advertising agencies. TV and radio ads for cigarettes were banned as far back as 1971. But the tobacco companies still spend $800 to $900 million a year to promote and visually hawk their products via magazines and newspapers. The campaigns often play on the fears of smokers by filling slick pages with low-tar claims. The standard ads depict athletic and attractive types seemingly engaged in a healthful pursuit— smoking. No doubt the portrayal of cigarette brandishers as sophisticated, daring and sexy influences many unthinking people to take up the habit.

In an official government report, the Department of Health and Human Services (formerly HEW) found that the ad agencies also concentrate on one special target audience. The Report:

> In recent years, advertising in the United States has been directed specifically towards the women's market, with themes as diverse as the emancipation of women, the first woman (Biblical reference), romantic love, and the independent single woman. Most girl smokers have a positive impression of the individuals pictured in cigarette advertisements. The latter are seen as attractive, enjoying themselves, well dressed, sexy, young, and healthy.
>
> Thus, cigarette companies have been successful in creating a sense of mystery, sophistication, and power around the behavior of smoking.

You need only look at some typical pages in Sunday supplements and women's magazines. A characteristic ad shows a sun-tanned young couple at their *al fresco* picnic table. "Benson & Hedges & Weekends & Me" reads the headline. "Because the pleasure lasts longer..." In another ad, a young woman is on the phone, her B&H grasped between her fingers. She may be talking to her boyfriend. ("Because the pleasure lasts longer.") "I'm more satisfied!" screams another ad while a competing brand simply displays two cross-country skiers silhouetted against the snow.

Deceptive Images

Playboy magazine, which reaps $12 million a year from the tobacco firms, often contains ads picturing hiking and camping scenes, or a mountain climber puffing a Camel ("Where A Man Belongs"), and the macho Marlboro cowboys. Cigarettes are shown in romantic last-fading sunlight fishing scenes. The burning stub in the angler's mouth is one of the "Vantage Pleasures." Barclay cigarettes' ads say: "The Pleasure is back." The lit-up weed is often the symbol for the sociable event among Beautiful People: you see radiant, sensuous women hugging a menthol brand, or one more young beauty holding up her Benson & Hedges in a full-page of *Gourmet* magazine. The latter is not rendering a service to its readers; genuine food connoisseurs know that their taste buds would be deadened by smoke; the world's Gourmet Societies shun cigarettes.

Snaring New Cigarette Customers

Although the industry denies it, much of the barrage is aimed at a younger, more naive reader. After all, models in their early twenties appeal to teenagers; so do some of the activities associated with smoking, like water-skiing or snow-skiing. The ad scenes hammer home a false health and glamor message; one Winston ad even suggests that smoking is part of becoming mature. "When your taste grows up," says a young lumberjack in a Winston ad, "Winston out-tastes them all." (In the same sense, the "You've come a long way, baby," is aimed at the liberated woman, telling her that it's okay to light up; after all, she makes her own decisions now and can do whatever she pleases.)

The ads are seductive and ingenious. "They're the state of the art," says one insider who wants to remain anonymous. "We advertise something that really isn't needed or wanted and that is bad for your health. Of course, we have large research departments. We use psychologists. And we appeal to the viewer's subconscious."

In a confidential ad agency report, one executive admitted that there are "not any real positive qualities and attributes in a cigarette. Advertising must therefore give smokers a rationale..." and sometimes the rationale can be very basic. In their campaign for Viceroy, the agency's theme was simple enough: "If it feels good, do it; if it feels good, smoke it..."

The cigarettes' names reflect this philosophy, too. "Lark," "Players," "Lucky Strike" all seem light-hearted, insouciant.

Dr. D.L. Geisinger, a psychologist, made a special study of cigarette names, analyzing what's behind them. He says the brand names are designed to influence you. Names such as True, Real and Merit are designed to make you feel good about smoking. He also says, "The names of some cigarettes cluster around associations of royalty and aristocracy (Kent, Montclair, Viceroy, Regency, Carlton, Parliament, Raleigh, Marlboro, Tareyton, Winston, Chesterfield), in order, I suppose, to make you feel more dignified and 'respectable' when you light up."

The FTC (Federal Trade Commission) remains highly critical of the ads themselves. In a recent analysis of cigarette advertising, the Commission's investigators pointed to the "rugged, vigorous, attractive, healthy-looking people living energetic lives full of success and athletic achievement..." The FTC's conclusion: "Not only are most cigarette advertisements filled with this rich, thematic imagery, many may even more strongly divert or distract attention away from the health consequences of smoking by portraying smoking as compatible with or, at least, as associated with a wide range of rigorous athletic or other strenuous activities. It is possible that these ads make it more difficult for the health warning to be effective and may further increase the possibility of deception.

The message is driven home in magazines like *Time* (which earns $15 million a year from the tobacco companies), *TV Guide* ($20 million) and assorted other money-hungry publications. On the other hand, the *Reader's Digest, The Christian Science Monitor* and *The New Yorker* have resisted the financial lure. They get along very well, too.

The public's bombardment with "smoking-is-fun" messages doesn't stop with magazines and papers; there are also the huckstering direct-mail campaigns, billboards, posters on trains, subways, bus terminals and airports, and small placards in taxis and, occasionally, on the back of ski-lift chairs. Naturally, advertisements never show the dark side of the cigarette, only the merry, sexy scenes. (The Swedish government is tougher on their agencies: the ads must depict cigarette packages against neutral backgrounds. See Chapter 14.)

Death rates by inhalation patterns
Rate per 100,000

Age	Degree of inhalation			
	None	*Slight*	*Moderate*	*Deep*
45-54	824	859	974	1,021
55-64	1,868	2,376	2,351	2,689
65-74	3,994	5,029	5,300	6,411

Source: U.S. Government Printing Office

Although the tobacco industry was kicked out of the American TV-studios a decade ago, the television ads are back via cigarette-sponsored sports events. A tobacco firm may spend as much as $80 million to launch a new brand. In fact, the cigarette makers will soon shell out $1 billion a year to manipulate you, and at the same time earn themselves handsome tax benefits that come out of the taxpayers' pockets.

Cigarette makers also use their power with other "Please-Smoke" messages. Consider: Free samples are given away to place the product in your hands.

Major tobacco companies sponsor special events to promote their wares to large audiences. Examples? The Marlboro Cup Horse Race, the Virginia Slims' Tennis Tournament, the Winston Cup Auto Race, the Raleigh-sponsored National Bowling Council Championship, the Kool Jazz Festival, and More's Ebony Fashion Fair. All of these have made an impact on the innocent via the otherwise forbidden TV-tube and the print media.

During the early eighties, the R.J. Reynolds Tobacco Company began to plug the "Camel Expeditions," a series of rugged adventures.

R.J. Reynolds' involvement, to the tune of more than $1 million in advertising and promotion, is an effort to extend the use of a famous trademark, the Camel cigarette brand logo.

"Just as companies have sponsored sporting events and concerts to enhance the image of their products with the public, we are getting involved in adventure travel," says a Reynolds' Tobacco official. The ads tout river-rafting scenes. "You enter the unknown," reads the ad copy. "When you've lived in the primitive, you'll discover how much more of a man you've become." End of macho message. Camel also promotes a mountain climbing expedition and other outings. You almost think that the cigarette company has gone "National Geographic" style.

Jackie Rogers, founder of SmokEnders, makes an intelligent comment about these goings-on, "The cigarette companies have done a superb marketing job," says Ms. Rogers. "Can you imagine persuading millions of people to do something that costs a lot of money, that is kind of dirty, that makes them smell bad, that offends friends and relatives, that causes gagging and coughing and is a messy nuisance and might kill them?"

The super-strong U.S. cigarette industry often flexes its corporate muscles. In the late seventies, for instance, a British TV-company had the excellent idea of filming some "Marlboro types" who died of lung cancer. The TV cameras zeroed in on a former cattle-brand inspector and on an afflicted rodeo rider, among others. They called their film, *Death in the West* and showed it to some 16 million viewers in Europe. The makers of Marlboro cigarettes at once mobilized their international attorneys, in an attempt to stop the show from being aired. They were unsuccessful. What with retail sales of some $17 billion a year, the industry is rich and wants to stay that way.

Inside the Tobacco Institute

Most of the cigarette makers' legwork is done by the "Tobacco Institute," which Senator Edward Kennedy once called the "most effective lobby on Capitol Hill." It may also be among the most influential lobbies. One of its directors, for instance, is a former North Carolina congressman.

The Institute was founded by the tobacco industry "to foster public understanding of the smoking and health controversy" and "to build public knowledge of the historic role of tobacco and its place in the national economy." The lobby publishes a number of brochures, booklets, and articles, which attempt to refute the fact that smoking is a major health hazard.

Through its main office in Washington, D.C. and its field representatives, the Tobacco Institute also provides public speakers who present the industry's case before service club audiences and over radio and television stations around the country. The Institute's most powerful role is that of a lobbyist for the tobacco industry in local, state and national legislatures. Lobbying pressure by the Institute has defeated a number of legislative and regulatory attempts to restrict the marketing and advertising of cigarettes and protect the rights of nonsmokers.

In one of its booklets, the Institute urges smokers and nonsmokers to help defeat the current movement to ban smoking in public places by "using facts such as those presented in this publication" to write letters to the editor complaining about smoking restrictions; to write and call local, state and national legislatures voicing opposition to nonsmoking bills or ordinances; to tell others about the potential dangers of such laws; and to call on the Tobacco Institute for help, "if smoking restrictions become an issue in your area."

A Lobby That Can Twist Political Arms

The Tobacco Lobby refers to leaders in the anti-smoking movement as "zealots" and "fanatics" who are trying to cripple the tobacco industry, put millions of people out of jobs and control public behavior by taking away the individual freedom of millions of Americans who enjoy smoking. Statistics on the health hazards are labeled by the Institute as "deceptive" propaganda.

The Lobby often insists that there is no proof that smoking causes any disease. "There are only statistical associations," says the Lobby. The Tobacco Institute channels funds to important legislators, contributes large sums to political campaigns and tries to influence members of both the House and Senate. Whenever states attempt to raise tobacco taxes, this powerful Lobby is there straining against it.

Dr. Sidney M. Wolfe, director of the Health Research Group, says the Tobacco Institute has "completely paralyzed Washington in terms of any significant ability to regulate cigarettes."

Some of the greatest battles were fought by the Tobacco Institute against the Department of Health during Joseph Califano's regime. The secretary of HEW—now the Department of Health and Human Services—had strong feelings about tobacco. He called it "Public Health Enemy Number One." He mounted an effective anti-cigarette campaign, which included personal letters to some 16,000 school superintendents.

The Lobby didn't take his efforts lightly and countered, among other measures, with the printing of bumper stickers that read, "Califano Is Dangerous to My Health." In private, the former HEW chief was told by a leading politician, "You're driving the tobacco people crazy. These guys are vicious. They're out to destroy you!" As it happened, former president Carter didn't share Califano's anti-tobacco ideas. Although Carter's own father—a four-pack-a-day man—had died painfully from lung cancer, Jimmy Carter sided with the tobacco states whose votes he needed. For this and various other reasons Califano, a cabinet officer, was forced to resign.

The U.S. Government and Cigarettes

Indeed, what about the U.S. government? Historically, the "Office on Smoking and Health" has been underfinanced, compared with the Tobacco Lobby. Moreover, the Feds collect taxes on cigarettes to the tune of some $2 billion a year. A decline in smoking would reduce the take. And while the Tobacco Institute's self-serving statements must be taken with a grain of ash, the Lobby speaks the truth about one government worry. What if America's tobacco workers become unemployed? In such states as North Carolina and Kentucky, for instance, tobacco products are essential for economic survival. Actually, more than 500,000 farm families in some twenty states depend on the tobacco crop for their livelihood. (For many years, these farmers have also received a government subsidy for growing tobacco.)

Production and prices of tobacco 1947–49 to 1978				
Year	Total acreage, thousands of acres	Unit yield pounds per acre	Production millions of pounds	Unit price cents per pound	Total crop value millions of dollars
1947–49 1,676		1,208	2,019	45.9	926
1955 1,495		1,466	2,193	53.2	1,166
1960 1,142		1,703	1,944	60.9	1,184
1965 977		1,898	1,855	65.1	1,207
1970 898		2,122	1,906	72.9	1,389
1978 949		2,135	2,026	132.4	2,682

Source: U.S. Department of Agriculture

As a result of these pressures, Uncle Sam has done almost nothing against the Cigarette Forces. But Califano, now a lawyer and private citizen, doesn't feel beaten. In his recent autobiography, he expressed his credo with candor. "Smoking cigarettes is suicide in slow motion," Califano wrote. "And the cigarette industry sells a product that has killed more Americans more painfully than have all our wars and all our traffic accidents combined."

4

The Health Factors

The operation is in progress. The surgeons wear sky-blue gowns, even blue gloves. An intense light bathes the masked nurses, the anesthesiologists and the patient's chest.

Instruments and clamps clink. A glinting rib spreader moves into action. At last, one lung is visible, a pulsating mass, tar-blackened by decades of cigarette smoking. The lung's lower lobe bristles with a white-grey area the size of a golf-ball. The thoracic surgeon's scalpel descends, draws blood, begins to work on the cancerous organ. The lobe eventually comes out.

Draped in towels, the patient—a man in his early forties—is lucky. The cancer was caught in its early stages. It affected only part of a lung. Including the biopsy and the complicated OR (operating room) procedure, the operation took almost five hours. The surgeons are tired; the patient's oncologist will be satisfied.

A fictitious case? Not at all. I witnessed the scalpel's handiwork on film, in vivid, memory-riveting colors. The occasion? A stop-smoking group's first session. The OR scene impressed me so much—especially the blood—that after years of slavery, I was tobacco free within two days after seeing that movie.

The young man in the film was indeed lucky. According to the latest statistics, lung carcinoma kills more men ages thirty-five to fifty-four than any other form of cancer. Because more women have been smoking for the past two decades, lung cancer may, within two years, become the number one killer of all women. (At present, breast cancer still leads.)

The most recent Surgeon General's Report points out one more important finding: Lung cancer rarely hits nonusers. In one study of 8,000 cases at a VA hospital, 98 percent of them were smokers.

It's the cigarette fiend's disease. Might air pollution be an additional cause? Not so. Several religious sects who live in large polluted cities, but are not allowed to smoke, rarely come down with lung problems.

Not long ago, Dr. Otto Gsell, a Swiss, happened to make a medical survey of a small remote Alpine hamlet. Why did the villagers have an unusually high incidence of lung cancer? The air was pure in this valley! After some additional interviews, the cause became as evident to Dr. Gsell as the blue Swiss sky. The farmers were all life-long smokers. Tobacco had done in many of them.

It's the European and North American chain smoker's *self*-pollution that brings him or her to the OR with carcinoma. The age at which people start smoking is relevant, too. Men who began before the age of fifteen suffer the most ill effects; historically, this group has a five times higher death rate from malignant lung tumors than those who only start their habit at age twenty-five.

Unfortunately, each year in the U.S. alone, about 120,000 people die needlessly from the disease. This includes many celebrities. The late Walt Disney and broadcaster Edward Murrow were cigarette smokers. Tallulah Bankhead and Duke Ellington also died from lung cancer. Singer Enrico Caruso died at forty-eight after a long bout with the disease. More recently, the great Italian director-actor Vittorio De Sica departed this way.

He was hooked on two high-tar packs a day almost to the end. If you consume that many cigarettes, your demise from lung trouble is twenty-six times more likely than if you are a nonsmoker. (Especially if you start young and inhale.) Certain professions—asbestos or rubber workers, uranium miners, oil refinery people—run even greater risks if they also insist on inhaling the lethal cigarette fumes. Keep in mind that it takes from ten to twenty years of puffing away at a steady pace to wind up with a case of bronchogenic carcinoma. And even then, some people are spared; they are just less susceptible. Of the others who get sick with lung cancer only fifteen in one hundred patients are cured.

It seems obvious that prevention is better than self-destruction. And in the last Report, the Surgeon General actually held out some hope to the addicts. His words make sense. "Smoking cigarettes with lower yields of 'tar' and nicotine reduces the risk of lung cancer and, to some extent, improves the smoker's chance for longer life, provided there is no compensatory increase in the amount smoked. However, the benefits are minimal in comparison with giving up cigarettes entirely. The single most effective way to reduce hazards of smoking continues to be that of quitting entirely."

However, for some people that is much easier said than done. In order to be able to quit you have to identify why you smoke, give yourself a motivation to quit and then start and stick with a cessation program.

Test 2
What Do You Think the Effects of Smoking Are?

For each statement, circle the number that shows how you feel about it. Do you strongly agree, mildly agree, mildly disagree, or strongly disagree? *Important: Answer every question.*

	strongly agree	mildly agree	mildly disagree	strongly disagree
A. Cigarette smoking is not nearly as dangerous as many other health hazards.	1	2	3	4
B. I don't smoke enough to get any of the diseases that cigarette smoking is supposed to cause.	1	2	3	4
C. If a person has already smoked for many years, it probably won't do him much good to stop.	1	2	3	4
D. It would be hard for me to give up smoking cigarettes.	1	2	3	4
E. Cigarette smoking is enough of a health hazard for something to be done about it.	4	3	2	1
F. The kind of cigarette I smoke is much less likely than other kinds to give me any of the diseases that smoking is supposed to cause.	1	2	3	4
G. As soon as a person quits smoking cigarettes he begins to recover from much of the damage that smoking has caused.	4	3	2	1
H. It would be hard for me to cut down to half the number of cigarettes I now smoke.	1	2	3	4
I. The whole problem of cigarette smoking and health is a very minor one.	1	2	3	4
J. I haven't smoked long enough to worry about the diseases that cigarette smoking is supposed to cause.	1	2	3	4
K. Quitting smoking helps a person to live longer.	4	3	2	1
L. It would be difficult for me to make any substantial change in my smoking habits.	1	2	3	4

HOW TO SCORE:
1. Enter the numbers you have circled to the Test 2 questions in the spaces below, putting the number you have circled to Question A over line A, to Question B over line B, etc.
2. Total the 3 scores across on each line to get your totals. For example, the sum of your scores over lines A, E, and I gives you your score on *Importance*—lines B,F, and J give the score on *Personal Relevance*, etc.

Totals

____ + ____ + ____ = ____
A   E   I   Importance

____ + ____ + ____ = ____
B   F   J   Personal Relevance

____ + ____ + ____ = ____
C   G   K   Value of Stopping

____ + ____ + ____ = ____
D   H   L   Capability for Stopping

Scores can vary from 3 to 12. Any score 9 and above is *high;* any score 6 and below is *low*. From the Department of Health, Education and Welfare publication, *Smoker's Self-Testing Kit*, 1975.

Lung Cancer: The Symptoms

According to the specialists of the American Cancer Society, the disease often develops without drama. The first symptoms may be an ordinary cough, a wheeze, a slight pain, easy to shrug off as unimportant. A heavy smoker is used to that special cough, even to some shortness of breath. So why think that anything is amiss?

The most common symptom is a cough, which is likely to occur when a growing cancer blocks an airway. The smoker coughs as if trying to get rid of a foreign object stuck in the lung. In some cases, the sputum contains streaks of blood.

The victim's second most frequent complaint is chest pain. It occurs as a persistent ache. Pathologists claim that every chain-smoker develops abnormal cells in the airways. These are cells that can be easily seen under the microscope. It makes sense that even the healthiest respiratory system will in time rebel against the invasion of tobacco gasses and other irritating particles.

Some resulting medical problems are now known as COPD, an abbreviation for "chronic obstructive pulmonary disease." This includes the longtime smoker's scourge of chronic bronchitis, which causes plenty of coughing, hacking and spitting. Actually, cases of this ailment have turned up among young people. In the same sense, and also part of COPD, smoking is the main culprit for "emphysema," a disease that destroys the lungs' air sacs.

Emphysema

Emphysema mainly strikes smokers. One of the symptoms is difficult breathing. In a now much-quoted talk, a former HEW director spoke of "emphysema victims literally choking to death." And in a movie at one smoking cessation program, the camera ventured into the hospital room of an elderly patient who was gasping his last breaths. He had not been a pipe or cigar man but had smoked his favorite cigarette brand for some fifty years. Eighty percent of these modern emphysema sufferings are because of smoking and some 17,000 Americans die from the disease every year.

Many victims are unaware of anything seriously wrong until most of their lung function is already impaired. Respiratory infections may also occur, followed by long periods of "not feeling up to par." Finally, coughing spells and shortness of breath force the patient to seek medical advice.

Unless it becomes chronic, bronchitis is less serious and can be cured. All the same, Mark Twain died of it. (Twain's quip is still famous: "To cease smoking, is the easiest thing I ever did. I ought to know because I've done it a hundred times!")

The U.S. government's pulmonary experts tell us that if in doubt, you can test your lung capacity at home. Light a match and hold it about six inches from your face. Then with your mouth wide open, blow it out. If you can't blow it out, see your doctor, immediately. Using a simple machine called a spirometer, your doctor can measure the ventilatory function, test the lung's capacity and resilience and, most importantly, how efficiently you can exhale. Combined with a thorough physical examination, the spirometer can help reveal whether or not you have early signs of a breathing disorder.

Consider the words of Dr. Tommy Koefoed, who for many years was a pulmonary therapist in Greenland and now runs smoking cessation clinics in Colorado. "We never saw a case of lung cancer in Greenland. Not even one!" says Dr. Koefoed. "The reason became clear enough. Greenlanders didn't know about cigarettes until 1945 when the first cartons arrived. After a twenty-year grace period, we saw our first lung cancer case. The following year, we had five cases. Now there are many more. We know now that the disease is almost entirely one of smokers."

Buerger's Disease

Physicians have found some other contemporary developments that include Buerger's disease. "Of 100 patients, 99 are smokers," states a German physician. What are the symptoms? Your extremeties feel cold when they shouldn't. You also get cramps in your legs.

The reasons are simple, of course. Smoking reduces the oxygen supply to your muscles, constricts your arteries and inflames your blood vessels. Ironically, Buerger's Disease often afflicts people in their twenties and thirties. If they continue to ingest nicotine, over their doctor's objections, the circulation to the legs and feet may get defective enough for a full-blown case of gangrene. Of course, this is rare, but possible. Amputation could be the result.

Arterial Problems and Cigarettes

Researchers have also discovered that hardening of the arteries (known as "arteriosclerosis") can be hastened by the weed. Cigarettes, alas, raise your cholesterol level; the nicotine stimulates your adrenaline output, which in turn sends fatty acids scurrying through your blood. At an autopsy, pathologists examined the arteries of heavy cigarette smokers. The scientists found a greater number of fatty plaques. And worse luck: in people who enjoy their daily forty cigarettes, the smoker's blood vessel walls had thickened and shrunk suspiciously. When this happens the tight, fat-clogged arteries struggle with their delivery of enough blood to the brain, which can cause strokes.

Unfortunately, there is more. The crime sheet also lists your favorite brands as the co-culprit in various often-fatal coronary ailments. Cigarettes and stress drive up your blood pressure, thus propelling a person toward cardiovascular trouble and a possible heart attack.

The above is not meant to alarm you or to concern the "occassional" one-Kent-after-dinner type, but applies only to the true nicotine addict. Keep in mind that one pack a day amounts to some 70,000 heart-pushing puffs a year. And one pack a day can subject a smoker's heart to 10,000 more beats than the nonsmoker's. If you consider all that extra stimulation for twenty years, you can easily see what might happen. According to the Surgeon General, smokers suffer three times more heart attacks than non-smokers, a possible result of this overexertion by the heart.

Some New Research on Heart Trouble

One major piece of detective work by the American Medical Association's "Committee for Research on Tobacco and Health" concerned the link between cigarettes and heart problems. The research project cost $15 million and the resulting 365 pages laid it all on the line. "Smoking not only constitutes a grave danger to individuals with preexisting coronary diseases," wrote the AMA doctors. "The combination of nicotine and the smoker's temporary lack of oxygen can also cause irreversible heart damage in healthier, younger individuals." Of course, this situation is aggravated by a sit-too-much lifestyle and bad eating habits.

For the innocent, these are the symptoms of trouble in your all-important heart pump:

> Prolonged, squeezing pain or unusual discomfort in the center of the chest, right under the breastbone. Pain may spread to the shoulder, arm, neck or jaw. The pain or discomfort is often accompanied by sweating. Nausea, vomiting and shortness of breath may also occur. These symptoms may subside and then return. Sometimes these symptoms are preceded for weeks or months beforehand by increased nervous tension, worry, fatigue, sleeplessness, recurrent chest pain and heart palpitations. Each is a warning that needs attention from a doctor.

It is significant that the athletic Hannes Schneider, one of the great stars of the ski world, was a heart disease sufferer. A physically active person, he had come from Austria to the U.S. as a skiing instructor. He skied every day, but he also smoked to excess every day. A final myocardial infarction eventually claimed him. In the same sense, physicians blamed former president Johnson's long-time smoking habit for a worsening and eventually fatal heart condition. And dancer/director Bob Fosse, an inveterate smoker, has had his share of attacks.

In some cases, the disease lingers. In others, it's sudden death. In one important study by Dr. D.T. Nash, New York cardiologist, smokers wound up with a four-time greater chance to die suddenly. The only silver lining: you can improve your odds by quitting.

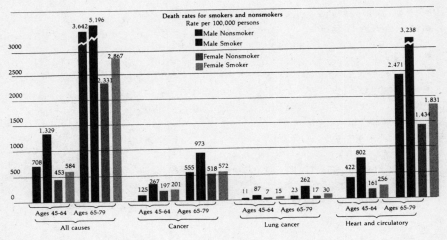

Death rates for smokers and nonsmokers
Rate per 100,000 persons

■ Male Nonsmoker
■ Male Smoker

▨ Female Nonsmoker
▨ Female Smoker

Source: U.S. Government Printing Office

A Medley of Illnesses and Problems

The same applies to some other important organs. You're more likely to keep your stomach lining intact if you don't reach for a Pall Mall or a Lucky Strike upon awakening, as I used to do. That first waker-upper can play havoc with your gastric system, and after enough nicotine abuse, could lead to an unpleasant peptic ulcer. Stomach cancer occurs twice as often in smokers than in abstainers. Some other vital organs, such as your pancreas and your kidneys, can also be mortally affected.

For years, a tennis partner of mine insisted on his daily double ration of Marlboros. "I've never been sick a day in my life," he would often tell me. One morning, while having his annual checkup, he asked his doctor about a puzzling matter. Why did he have blood in his urine?

As it happened, the cells in his bladder had gone haywire. A cystoscope exploration followed. Diagnosis: Malignant bladder tumor.

Physicians suspect that some of the cigarette's carcinogens in the blood stream eventually end up in the urine, where, after enough storage hours and enough years the bladder reacts adversely, as in my tennis partner's case.

Cause and effect must (and often do) play their part in this business of human deterioration. When I still smoked, old Dr. Cody, a dentist, would complain about my chronically red gums. I ignored his critique and continued the noxious habit. Result: a solid, drawn-out case of bleeding gingivitis, with loss of several teeth. At every exam, Dr. Cody would look deeply into my mouth, watching for telltale signs of oral cancer—white patches, persistent sores, tissues changing colors. After a gum operation, I stopped smoking forever. I escaped Sigmund Freud's fate: a sixteen-year ordeal of inner jaw scraping, thirty-two operations in all. The pain was excruciating at times, yet perversely, Dr. Freud continued this self-abuse to the end.

It's difficult to imagine how someone gets along without a tongue, the palate or deeper down, with the surgical loss of the esophagus (gullet). Smoker's laryngitis is less serious except when you're a politician; the inability to speak hurt Wendell Willkie, who could not address voters in the 1940 Presidential campaign.

The tissues of your larynx (which controls speech) are less than happy with the chemicals in your cigarettes; if you also drink much hard liquor, the combination can cause cancer in your voice box. Some years ago, a talented writer faced that particular surgery. He kept track of his thoughts and observations in an article that he aptly titled, "What The Cigarette Commercials Don't Show." In more sense than one, his was a throat-wrenching story.

It is true that the physicians of the eighties know a great deal more about these things than their peers of the sixties. The newest medical papers offer more cures and also sound more justified warnings.

Women have become a new target: every recent medical report piles up the evidence that women who take the pill and smoke more than twenty cigarettes a day take great risks. Doctors say that for nonsmokers of any age, the birth control pill by itself does not necessarily increase the possibility of a shorter life. But for women over forty who smoke heavily, the pill appears to be more chancy than any other contraceptive method. It seems that heavy tobacco use, plus the drug, will increase the chances of blood clotting. According to Joe Graedon, a respected pharmacologist, females who smoke and take the pill are seventy times more prone to get a heart attack. "Countless millions smoke like fiends," writes Graedon. "It is fair to assume that thousands of hypertensive women are literally taking their lives in their hands by using this form of contraception."

Even the drug merchants are aware of these dangers; in fact, since 1978, the Feds have demanded that pill packages carry a warning to women smokers.

The FDA message minces no words. "Cigarette smoking increases the risk of serious adverse effects on the heart and blood vessels from oral contraceptive use. The risk increases with age and with heavy smoking (fifteen or more cigarettes per day) and is quite marked in women over thirty-five years of age. Women who use oral contraceptives should not smoke."

None of this is meant to upset the reader. But these facts for women speak louder than the joyous Virginia Slim ads.

Item: Nicotine restricts blood vessels and breathing movements of unborn babies in women who smoke, while carbon monoxide reduces the oxygen level of their blood. This hinders normal growth so the babies weigh an average of six ounces less at birth than babies whose mothers are non-smokers. The weight is even lower for babies born at high altitudes.

Item: New statistics show a direct connection between smoking during pregnancy and the incidence of miscarriage, premature birth and stillbirth. Women who consume a pack or more of cigarettes a day during pregnancy suffer about a 50 percent greater risk of infant mortality.

Item: A long-term follow-up study shows that when the mothers were heavy smokers during pregnancy, by the age of seven their children had turned out shorter in stature, with a retarded reading ability and lower ratings on "social adjustment" than the children of nonsmoking mothers.

On the somewhat less serious side, a California skin specialist discovered that girls who smoke develop facial wrinkles much sooner in life. They are the ones with crows feet around their eyes at age twenty-five. Apparently the nicotine makes their vessels contract, and their cells and tissues do not get enough oxygen. All of which helps create more wrinkles sooner.

Heavy smoking apparently lowers testerone in male smokers. This may reduce the active sperm count and even lower sexual endurance. This has been the theory of Dr. Alton Ochsner, a surgeon and anti-tobacco advocate who also became well-known for his sexuality studies. One of his classic cases: a seventy-three-year-old male smoker who managed sexual relations only once every six months. Dr. Ochsner persuaded him to quit. Result? "Now he has sex three times a week!"

Dr. Ochsner was once asked if the seventy-three-year-old wasn't an isolated case. Did the male population really improve their sex lives if they got rid of the habit? Himself eighty-two at the time, the famed physician thought for a moment. Then he turned to his interviewer. "Many of my male patients will say that they now do better in the bedroom. Their wives know the difference, too. Yes, to stop smoking is the answer."

Hear, hear!

5

Why and How People Quit

A lone man's companion,
A bachelor's friend,
A hungry man's food,
A sad man's cordial,
A wakeful man's sleep,
And a chilly man's fire—
There's no herb like unto it under
    the canopy of heaven.

Thus wrote the English poet Charles Kingsley, an avid smoker who lived from 1819 to 1875. Ah, the poets have sung the praises even in Latin to the *Nicotiana tabacum*, to tobacco.

Extravagant multicolored magazine ads extol the virtues of smoking, the models forever suggesting pleasure. And oh, yes, I remember nostalgically those quiet moments with a cigarette *a deux*; in those days, romance still meant two heads together with two lighted stubs sending their silky aroma toward the sky.

The Chemist's List of Compounds

It took some years and the reading of many documents to learn the truth about how tobacco is grown (with nitrate fertilizers) and made (with paper that sends toxic selenium into your body). And I was alarmed to come upon a National Institute for Occupational Safety and Health report that identified a number of potential contaminants in tobacco products "including inorganic fluorides and mercury, lead, dinitro-ortho-creosol, formaldehyde, boron trifluoride, organotin, methyl parathion and carbaryl, and cyanide." Other harmful chemical agents in your cigarette include acetone, acrolein, aldehydes, cadmium, hydrogen sulfide, detones, lead, methyl nitrite, nitrogen dioxide and phenol.

You almost need to be a chemist to know all those nasty compounds, which are just a few among hundreds. The Institute also names arsenic, well-known from mystery novels as a subtle killer, and propane and butane as among the less healthy ingredients.

Of course, even the lay person knows that cigarettes impart a hefty dose of carbon monoxide. As you breathe it, you might keep in mind that carbon monoxide happens to be the favorite poison gas for people who want to commit suicide in closed garages. The officials of the American Lung Association, who should know such things, say that the colorless, odorless gas literally drives the oxygen out of your red blood cells. Carbon monoxide levels in the blood of cigarette addicts are four times higher than for those who abstain. For heavy smokers, this can sometimes be even fifteen times higher! Remember that carbon monoxide has a great affinity for your hemaglobin, and thus makes you anemic. Moreover, carbon monoxide likes to *remain* in your bloodstream. It is known to rob the human body of oxygen for as long as six hours after you've stubbed out your last cigarette. Worse yet, in chain smokers, carbon monoxide builds up. And up.

As if this were not all, radiation is an additional ingredient in that burning cigarette. According to a study by Dr. E.A. Martell, a National Center for Atmospheric Research chemist, radioactive particles stick to the lungs; radioactivity increases over the years with each hot smoke. In the end, the addict winds up with radiation doses that are reminiscent of what happens to miners in certain mines. Dr. Martell also discovered another trouble source: radioactive particles collect on the willing hairs of tobacco leaves. When these hairs burn at high temperatures, as they do in your cigarette at 1300 to 1600 degrees, the tobacco liberates tiny amounts of radioactive lead straight into your lungs. Naturally, inhaling makes all this worse. So does the bad custom of consuming a cigarette down to its butt.

The AMA meanwhile likes to point out that 90 percent of the fumes from cigarettes are gases—about a dirty dozen of them, including the ill-reputed carbon monoxide. These gases are all health hazards. The remainder of the smoke consists of nicotine and tars.

Cigarettes were always and foremost known for those tars. They accumulate in human lungs, acting as irritants and stirring up your cells. A pack a day means about 840 cubic centimeters of tar a year, or about 27 fluid ounces, i.e., just short of a quart. (The tars made names for themselves when brushed on mice. The creatures first shed their hair, then turned scaly, and at last developed warts, then tumors and died.) The evils of tar have been publicized for decades, and after enough turmoil, the cigarette companies finally took some interest in the matter. The folks at Reynolds Tobacco,

Phillip Morris *et al.* reduced the tar content of their products. Oddly enough, this just meant the real smokers had to take deeper puffs for their nicotine fix, and thus risked just as much damage as before. And, just as bad, low-tar cigarettes produce more nitrogen oxides.

Bear in mind that researchers point to still other elements such as pesticides, for instance, or the previously mentioned nerve-stimulating nicotine that changes your body chemistry in several ways and would kill you if it were injected.

Enough. You can fairly conclude that these poisons don't do much for your longevity. (Maybe that's why some 110,000 doctors have quit smoking during the last few years.) In the past, various animal experiments also shed a fascinating light on this business. Among the best-known scientific work was done under the auspices of the American Lung Association during the early seventies. The experiment consisted of a long-term study that involved almost 100 healthy dogs, beagles, to be exact.

The animals were given the equivalent of one to two packs a day. One control group of beagles was allowed to abstain. After 875 days, all the smoking dogs had tumors or showed other pathological changes. Some of them died, just as people would. And the nonsmokers? *All of them survived*, wagging their tails.

The Surgeon General's Determination

If the story above sounds convincing, the genuine dangers are spelled out on cigarette packages and in the corners of the glamorous ads,

WARNING:
The Surgeon General
Has Determined That
Cigarette Smoking
Is Dangerous To
Your Health

For many years now, some leading politicians have been aware that the message hasn't hit hard enough. They want to strengthen it: "Warning: Cigarette Smoking is Dangerous to your Health and May Cause Death from Cancer, Coronary Heart Disease, Chronic Bronchitis, Pulmonary Emphysema and Other Diseases." One consumer group even suggests a skull and crossbones with the message. Whatever happens, the U.S. Public Health Service labels smoking our "foremost cause of preventable disease and death."

Food for thought. And motivation to stop.

An involuntary look at the inside of a hospital can certainly do wonders to your resolve to quit. "That's exactly what happened to me," says Dr. Bryan Brook, a psychologist. "I was in a serious accident and had to go to the hospital. While I was there for ten days, I got to see people who had lip cancer, part of their lip removed, and other cigarette-related illnesses. And it scared the hell out of me. My father had just given me a brand new pipe. I had a little collection of seven to eight pipes worth about $60 or $70 and I literally threw them into the garbage can when I got home, because I figured I had one pair of lungs and one heart and that's it and I didn't want to wind up like these other people I'd seen. This personal scare made me quit smoking. This is the most powerful incentive to quit."

It was the possible adverse effect on my own health that influenced me to think seriously about smoking. These concerns propelled me toward the first serious stirrings that I needed to get the nicotine monkey off my back.

Why I Quit

Like many of my contemporaries, I enjoy life too much; I don't want to depart from these green shores any sooner than I have to. Death is to be avoided at all costs—especially when cigarettes can cost you your life. Living in health is all.

I first learned about the possibility of curtailed health some fifteen years ago. I was trying to play soccer with my young son Stephen. I used to be fast as a youngster, storming forward with the ball, dribbling it, kicking it deftly ahead of me as I raced toward the opponent's goal. But two decades of smoking had made short shrift of my soccer game. I couldn't run far or fast.

I had to catch my breath.

As everyone knows, this is impossible in a real soccer game. You have to keep moving. I tried but was halted by gasps and coughs.

I knew it then: I had found another good reason to quit. I wanted to play good soccer!

There were other motives connected with athletics. I'd always been a sports freak. My Camels—no filters, pure tobacco, pure tar, high carbon monoxide levels—were slowing me down as a daily jogger as well. Hiking was not as pleasurable as in my Camel-less youth. And imagine a long-time cross-country skier with black lungs and irritated bronchi! The long, steady strides become brief and sloppy. The glide doesn't succeed.

Puzzled about my lack of stamina, I turned to a physician at the Colorado University Pulmonary Center. "The average smoker has much less lung power," I was told, "and less stamina." In fact, I learned from a Gerontology study that my lung function had aged by ten years! If I could get off cigarettes, I would add a decade to my breathing apparatus.

Problems show up even more blatantly at high altitudes. I began skiing at age five. I skied almost every winter day during my early twenties. Later, while living in the Rockies, I was drawn to such magnificent ski meccas as Snowmass-at-Aspen, Winter Park, Alta, Snowbird, Arapahoe Basin. And to the grand Swiss resorts like Zermatt, Davos, Klosters. But my thirty-Camels-a-day had temporarily crippled me. When I tried to ski the long

Parsenn runs of Switzerland, my oxygen-starved lungs complained. The cigarettes made me cough so violently that other skiers inquired discreetly: Did I suffer from Tuberculosis?

I still kept smoking on the ski lift. Result? After three or four downslope ski turns, I had to stop for a rest. Yes, stop! Reason: I was gasping for air. The Virginia tobacco really affected a healthy pair of lungs.

Later, when I made up my mind to seek a way to quit, I attended a smoking clinic, where I was treated to a movie. It dealt with a young runner. Dramatically, you first see him circle the track three times at a fairly fast clip. The next week, after some steady cigarette consumption, the motion picture camera is there again. This time, the sixteen-year-old can get around the track just one time. After that—and this is a true account of an individual!—the young runner started coughing and spitting. The tobacco had cut his energy level to the bone. He was exhausted after a mere mile. Why should this be so? Well, the runner just wasn't getting enough oxygen.

Bob Mathias, one of those rare Olympic decathlon gold medalists, once affirmed his credo for all times and all athletes. "Athletes in top condition don't smoke. They can't afford to!" Mathias told an interviewer, adding, "When you are in competition, you only want fresh air in your lungs. Smoking cuts down on wind. And as an athlete you need wind as much as you need your legs."

This gold medalist's statement makes sense. So does Dr. K.H. Cooper's historic U.S. Air Force test of almost 1,000 young recruits at the Lackland Air Force base. Dr. Cooper, author of *Aerobics*, divided his young men into five groups: Those who never smoked, those who smoked and quit, those who smoked an average of less than ten cigarettes a day, those who smoked ten to thirty, and those who smoked thirty or more. He put his groups into his standard conditioning program.

Dr. Cooper explains that "at the beginning of training, only the never-smoked, as a group, made it into the good category on the 12-minute test. The stopped-smoking group was just slightly behind, and the other three groups, in nice, neat order, were three, four and five behind. This did not surprise us."

What's more, the nonsmoking recruits remained "comfortably" in first place. The thirty-cigarettes-a-day people came in last.

In a similar experiment in England, an almost identical story emerged from studying the results of a three-mile cross-country run at the Aldershot Army School. During the span of seven years the performance of almost 2,000 men was analyzed, in groups of heavy smokers, moderate smokers, nonsmokers.

The heavy smokers, 8 percent of the total, drew most of the last ten places. The moderate smokers got 83 percent of the last places. The nonsmokers, 18 percent of the total, took most of the firsts.

Naturally, any normally healthy and athletic person would want to remove such an obvious performance obstacle and quit this self-abuse. To be sure, all kinds of outdoor activities crank up the needed motivations. In my case, there was an additional dilemma: For years, I earned my living as an outdoor writer. I wrote much about mountain climbing. And I learned about the rock-scaling techniques from the experts, including a few climbers with illustrious records in the Tetons, the Alps and the Himalayas. For awhile, I'd switched to cigars. It was embarrassing (to say the least) when I turned up for my belays and rappels with a cigar clamped between my teeth! One of the experts soon pointed out that I was in the wrong place: Nylon ropes could be severely damaged by my lighted tobacco leaves.

I was risking the entire climbing party's lives. At this point, I did not walk—I ran—to the first available stop-smoking seminar.

There were other reasons as well. I'd become a much slower tennis player. A little extended exercise (even a swim) made me feel lousy, a reminder that even worse health may be in store at a later time. Indeed, for some people, the resolve to quit is made easiest by a physician.

A writer of my acquaintance with a nasty case of asthma called on his doctor. The physician made things easy, saying, "I ask you to quit cigarettes as of today!" The writer complied. A pending operation and the white beginnings of oral cancer can spook anyone sufficiently to seek out a cessation method.

Pressure From Others as a Reason to Stop

In some cases, not only the medical profession but your family does a little pushing.

Couples are good examples: if one spouse (or sexual partner) doesn't smoke, the other one—even a long-time addict—will soon feel the prods and barbs that push him or her toward ending the habit. It was true that my own children, their anti-cigarette knowledge bolstered at high school, pleaded and cajoled until I went off to seek quitting help. I listened to their logic: they wanted a *healthy* father; besides, a smoking elder gives a poor example to his or her offspring and thereby diminishes his or her authority.

One of the best-known children and parents' case histories was that of Joseph Califano, the former Secretary of Health, Education and Welfare during the Carter years. In a talk to SmokEnders, a group that helped him end the habit, Califano remembered:

> In the summer of 1975, I was talking with my son Joe about his birthday present. His birthday comes shortly after Christmas, and he has the problem of all children in this situation—not quite having a full birthday. I asked him what he wanted.
>
> "For you to quit smoking," Joe said. Since quitting smoking had only occasionally crossed my mind, I laughed and said, "No, seriously what would you like?"

"It really would be a great present if you'd quit smoking," Joe repeated.

The conversation trailed off into other things. But the thought stuck in my head. My smoking had increased to about three packs a day. When the Kents I smoked irritated my throat, I would switch to mentholated Salems to anesthetize it.

For several days I reflected on what my son had said. I thought of my own health and was reluctantly aware of the risk of cancer and heart attack. I began to think seriously about quitting.

After some postponements, Califano grabbed the bull by the horns and joined SmokEnders. The group lived up to its name. (See Chapter 7.)

Quitting Because of Religious Reasons

For some people, the route to health is altogether different. At first misguided, they are led back to normalcy with the aid of old-fashioned religion. The Mormons are not forbidden to smoke, but smoking breaks one of their Commandments. And anyone who regularly breaks a Mormon Commandment cannot hold any church office.

The Jehovah's Witnesses cannot be baptized (i.e., become church members) if they are smokers.

Church of the Nazarene members are forbidden to indulge in tobacco by church law, because "it defiles the house of the Holy Spirit."

If you happen to be a Seventh-Day Adventist, a Christian Scientist or a member of several other church groups, you are unlikely to continue smoking. You'll stop quickly after a brief experiment.

A religious person is taught that life should be considered a precious gift. The Bible teaches that your body is "the dwelling place of God"; you must not "defile, debase or destroy it."

The Holy Scriptures do not mention the poisonous nicotine and tars, but young Christians are well aware of the words in the Corinthians: "Surely you know," the Apostle Paul wrote, "that you are God's temple, where the Spirit of God dwells. Anyone who destroys God's temple will himself be destroyed by God, because the temple of God is holy; and that temple you are." (I Corinthians 3:16)

Another Bible passage adds these wise thoughts: "Health of the soul is better than all gold and silver and a sound body than immense revenues."

A Christian Scientist explains his church's position this way: "Destructive habits such as smoking *can* be healed through a Christian understanding of what God is. This gives people the self-respect that addiction often would take away."

According to Christian teaching, "Divine Love corrects and governs: and so makes it possible to shed a damaging habit. Many a Christian can find help through prayer. One Pastor suggests: "Tell God about your desire and your resolve. Open the door of your heart heavenward and the Holy

Spirit, flowing in, will bring you both strength and victory."

But what of the agnostic? The atheist? The only remotely religious person? Indeed, how about the resolve for the contemporary man or woman? What could be your reasons?

Cigarettes, the New Social Stigma

Unless they have already been named—i.e., the fear of illness and the drive toward perfect health—there are more reasons to quit. Especially for up-to-date people. According to several important new studies, many smokers quit because they are being socially rejected. One psychologist puts it this way: "In the 1980s, many people won't date a person who smokes; they won't go out to dinner with a person who smokes; and they won't even sit in the same room with a person who smokes. So the most important thing about giving up smoking today is *social acceptance*."

It is true that smoking has suddenly become out of date, something done by "older folks," by "stupid, passe persons." At many universities, smoking students are shunned by others; one group in Boulder, Colorado, even went so far as to unleash water pistols at smokers in the university cafeteria. In one engineering college, students even use vulgarity. They give out cards to smokers reading, "Let's make a deal! You don't smoke and I won't fart!" It's true that nonsmokers are more belligerent these days; you need only consider such new slogans as "Kissing a smoker is like licking a dirty ashtray."

The cigarette habit is seen as gauche by many people who count. Not long ago, for instance, Consumer Advocate Ralph Nader had to confer with a high government official, a woman, who supposedly dealt with polluting factories and auto emission standards. Nader later described the meeting to the press as "an outrage." It seems that the woman had been "chain-smoking" Marlboros through the entire conference. Nader was incensed. "You'd think she'd at least abstain for an hour while we're talking about pollution!"

Dr. Morris Chefetz, a psychiatrist with a special reputation for the smoking controversy, lectures to experts at numerous research centers. His viewpoint underlines that of others. "Smoking will eventually stop," says Dr. Chefetz. "Reason? It is no longer socially tolerated."

The above situation also shows up in contemporary fashion advertising. You seldom see a *Vogue* or *Harper's Bazaar* model with a cigarette holder or its contents. Cigarettes are just not chic anymore. Likewise, *Playboy's* famous bunnies must now live by the nonsmoking rule, at least while on duty. "Cigarettes just don't look good," says their manual. "And it damages the bunny image." In the same sense, you will no longer see many smokers among the gathered Sierra Club gang—the outdoors shakers and movers believe in wellness. Likewise, smoking isn't "in" at meetings of hiking clubs, mountain clubs, explorer societies (except those sponsored by Camel cigarettes), or gatherings of important physicists, chemists, pathologists. Doctors' conventions are notorious for their empty ashtrays.

The National Interagency Council on Smoking and Health sponsors a National Education Week on Smoking in January of each year. The American Heart Association has changed its focus from stopping adults from smoking to smoking prevention announcements on radio and TV program segments for children.

"We haven't been as strong, collectively, in Washington as we should have been," concedes the American Lung Association's managing director. He predicts a "new era" of collaboration between his group, the American Heart Association, and the American Cancer Society. The new spirit of cooperation in these groups emerged from the National Conference on Smoking and Health, sponsored by twenty-one government agencies and volunteer health organizations. The participants produced a preliminary antismoking "Blueprint for Action." Its proposals included stepping up research on the prenatal effects of smoking, charging full price on military bases for tobacco products, strengthening instruction on smoking in medical schools, and mobilizing the anti-cigarette cause in schools and hospitals.

Most of the organizations also feel it is time for at least increasing federal taxes on tobacco products, despite a laissez-faire attitude by the executive branch of the Federal government. However, a former HEW undersecretary of health downplayed the role of the government in favor of an increased effort by health groups. "Public attitudes toward smoking can be influenced tremendously if the heart, lung and cancer people can string together their common interests in getting people not to smoke."

The mounting tide of anti-smoking action has had a profound effect on the tobacco industry. However, that same action has come under increased attack from tobacco's foes. They say that they neither can nor will "turn the other cheek." The Tobacco Institute President reminds us that:

> The cigarette controversy has overflowed its traditional boundaries. We have become involved in controversies that are much broader than the effect of smoke on the nonsmoker. We are involved in civil rights, human rights, lifestyles. We are becoming involved in the controversy of individual rights versus government regulations. We are involved in environmental, occupational and national health policy. In the largest sense, we are becoming involved in the fundamental questions of American life and the role of government in relation to it.

Research is underway, both by the Federal Government and by the tobacco industry, to produce a tobacco which is even lower in tar and nicotine. There have been products on the market which are made of non-tobacco substances, such as vegetable leaves. While these "smokes" do not contain nicotine, they do produce tars, sometimes to a greater extent than regular cigarettes. Whether or not these tars can cause cancer has not yet been determined.

Not all popular brands of cigarettes have the same tar and nicotine yield. Some, particularly those with filter tips, have a lower tar and a lower nicotine content, or are lower in both elements than other brands. The smoker who chooses brands with the lowest tar and nicotine yield can reduce his or her exposure to the harmful effects of smoking, provided the person does not compensate by smoking more.

Recently, The Tobacco Working Group, a part of the National Cancer Institute, was set up as a special task force to try to make cigarettes less hazardous. The group, including Department of Agriculture specialists and scientists from cigarette companies, helped develop new types of tobacco which were very low in tar and nicotine. It has also created cigarettes with fewer invisible poisonous "gases," particularly carbon monoxide, nitrogen oxides and hydrogen cyanide, implicated in smokers' heart attacks, chronic bronchitis and emphysema.

Public acceptance of low "tar" cigarettes will accelerate in the future. Cigarette companies will be competing heavily for the market of new low "tar" and nicotine brands. The R. J. Reynolds Tobacco Company budgeted $50 million in a single year to promote their low "tar" and nicotine brand, "Real."

The Congressional ban on televised cigarette ads came after the companies themselves had shown their willingness to stop such advertising. The ban brought to an end a period of three and one-half years when broadcasters carrying cigarette advertising were required to provide a significant amount of time to the health hazards of smoking. Gone are the days when the concern about the health consequences of cigarette smoking were overshadowed by TV commercials that depicted cigarette smoking as an aesthetically pleasing pastime.

But in spite of the grassroots support of nonsmoking as a lifestyle, the government's attitude toward tobacco is a study in contrasts. On one hand, Uncle Sam has banished tobacco commercials from television and required that tobacco products carry the U.S. Surgeon General's tepid warning that smoking is dangerous to health. On the other hand, it has provided tobacco price supports since 1938, steadily increasing the amount to the present $65 million, including an allotment of $24 million in loans for shipment of tobacco to underprivileged nations under the Food for Peace program. Then, when former president Carter made a well-publicized visit to tobacco country in North Carolina he said that he saw "no incompatibility" between annual price supports for tobacco farmers and pursuit of a "good health" program.

Additional subsidies to the tobacco industry—in the form of low-interest federal loan programs and government grading of tobacco—come to over

$30 million in a typical year in addition to a little-known $117 million in federally guaranteed loans to foreign manufacturers and nations with state-controlled tobacco industries for purchases of American tobacco.

Farms with cigarette tobacco allotments and those growing tobacco, 1977

State	Farms with allotments	Average allotment	Farms growing tobacco	Average size of farmed land
	Number	Acres	Number	Acres
Alabama	268	2.3	100	5.5
Florida	7,106	1.9	1,400	8.5
Georgia	25,330	2.7	5,000	13.0
Indiana	9,874	0.8	5,000	1.5
Kentucky	166,233	1.2	103,000	1.9
Maryland	2	2	3,000	7.7
Missouri	1,492	2.1	1,000	2.6
North Carolina	134,018	3.2	52,000	7.6
Ohio	11,771	1.2	7,600	1.3
South Carolina	23,907	2.9	6,000	11.3
Tennessee	104,704	0.9	62,000	1.1
Virginia	43,673	2.1	21,000	3.8
West Virginia	4,253	1.0	3,000	0.5
Total	532,629	1.9	270,100	3.5

Source: U.S. Department of Agriculture

Perhaps Congress should be urged to place the interests of 218 million Americans above the interests of six major cigarette-producing companies by passing legislation to:

1. Replace the federal excise tax of 8¢ a pack with an increased graduated uniform tax based on tar and nicotine content—a financial incentive to smoke low tar/nicotine cigarettes which would also curb cigarette bootlegging and increase tax revenues to the states.
2. Phase out tobacco price-supports over ten years; full payment to farmers for not growing tobacco; research into nonharmful tobacco uses and alternative crops, such as grains from which to distill alcohol for "gasohol" to help solve the energy problem.
3. Enact into law the Federal Trade Commission's recommended health warning label: "Warning: Cigarette Smoking Is Dangerous to Health, and May Cause Death From Cancer, Coronary Heart Disease, Chronic Bronchitis, Pulmonary Emphysema and Other Diseases."
4. Direct the Food and Drug Administration to regulate tobacco products, including the additives in cigarettes.

Also a comprehensive program by the Department of Health and Human Services and its numerous agencies is recommended and could include priority of funds for public education, anti-smoking advertising, a study of nicotine's addictive qualities and regulation of the tar/nicotine and carbon monoxide content of tobacco products by the Food and Drug Administration.

The influence of tobacco interests over Congress began in 1906 when it voted to declassify nicotine as an addictive drug to make certain that tobacco would not fall under the Food and Drug Administration. The tobacco lobby has successfully blocked every attempt at regulation and has seen to it that more than 150 regulatory bills were buried in committee.

With sentiment against smoking gathering momentum, the effectiveness of the large and powerful tobacco lobby is beginning to erode. A few months ago the Tobacco Institute, the voice of the American cigarette manufacturers, reported that there were forty-two bills in Congress that could be considered anti-tobacco.

As Representative James P. Johnson (Republican, Colorado)—himself a smoker—said after he introduced a bill to drop tobacco from Food for Peace: "There is no justification to support production of a poison."

Meanwhile, the cigarette industry remains basically unregulated and unaccountable to any agency of government for the content of its products or the health consequences of their use. The industry is seeking to increase the number of smokers by spending nearly half a billion dollars annually on advertising cigarettes while the Federal Government continues to support tobacco production and distribution.

Ceasing to Be a Slave

Of course, the reading of the latest Surgeon General's Report is convincing enough to get off the nicotine habit. But the search for other compelling must-quit motivations isn't too difficult.

The need for self-mastery seems to appear high on many lists, too.

Buddha told us in the fifth century B.C. that "though one should conquer a thousand men a thousand times, he who conquers himself has the more glorious victory." And Seneca, the Roman philosopher, wrote in 63 A.D. that "most powerful is he who has himself in his own power."

No one wants to be a slave to a habit. One anonymous American recalls candidly how, after being hooked for years, he finally, angrily, came to the conclusion to chuck the addiction: "The successful cigarette-quitting process started when I became thoroughly disgusted with myself upon realizing that I was being controlled by an addiction. The fact that I was unable to quit smoking made me angry. Was I not bigger than a filthy, debilitating habit? Didn't I hate those cigarette hangovers after a night out? Were those damned cigarettes bigger than me?" In the same sense, an Englishwoman told an interviewer that she considers herself "weakwilled" or she would be able to "toss off her addiction to nicotine."

Self-mastery yields a feeling of strength and self-confidence. It obviously imparts self-esteem. You did it! You were able to decide for yourself, to control part of your destiny. Quitting reestablishes self-respect. It is a sign of strength; it is to be admired by others as well.

Test 3
Why Do You Smoke?

Here are some statements made by people to describe what they get out of smoking cigarettes. How *often* do you feel this way when smoking them? Circle one number for each statement.
Important: Answer every question.

	always	frequently	occasionally	seldom	never
A. I smoke cigarettes in order to keep myself from slowing down.	5	4	3	2	1
B. Handling a cigarette is part of the enjoyment of smoking it.	5	4	3	2	1
C. Smoking cigarettes is pleasant and relaxing.	5	4	3	2	1
D. I light up a cigarette when I feel angry about something.	5	4	3	2	1
E. When I have run out of cigarettes I find it almost unbearable until I can get them.	5	4	3	2	1
F. I smoke cigarettes automatically without even being aware of it.	5	4	3	2	1
G. I smoke cigarettes to stimulate me, to perk myself up.	5	4	3	2	1
H. Part of the enjoyment of smoking a cigarette comes from the steps I take to light up.	5	4	3	2	1
I. I find cigarettes pleasurable.	5	4	3	2	1
J. When I feel uncomfortable or upset about something, I light up a cigarette.	5	4	3	2	1
K. I am very much aware of the fact when I am not smoking a cigarette.	5	4	3	2	1
L. I light up a cigarette without realizing I still have one burning in the ashtray.	5	4	3	2	1
M. I smoke cigarettes to give me a "lift."	5	4	3	2	1
N. When I smoke a cigarette, part of the enjoyment is watching the smoke as I exhale it.	5	4	3	2	1
O. I want a cigarette most when I am comfortable and relaxed.	5	4	3	2	1
P. When I feel "blue" or want to take my mind off cares and worries, I smoke cigarettes.	5	4	3	2	1
Q. I get a real gnawing hunger for a cigarette when I haven't smoked for a while.	5	4	3	2	1
R. I've found a cigarette in my mouth and didn't remember putting it there.	5	4	3	2	1

Totals

___	+	___	+	___	=	_____
A		G		M		Stimulation
___	+	___	+	___	=	_____
B		H		N		Handling
___	+	___	+	___	=	_____
C		I		O		Pleasurable Relaxation
___	+	___	+	___	=	_____
D		J		P		Crutch: Tension Reduction
___	+	___	+	___	=	_____
E		K		Q		Craving: Psychological Addiction
___	+	___	+	___		
F		L		R		Habit

HOW TO SCORE:
1 . Enter the numbers you have circled to the Test 3 questions in the spaces below, putting the number you have circled to Question A over line A, to Question B over line B, etc.
2 . Total the 3 scores on each line to get your totals. For example, the sum of your scores over lines A, G, and M gives you your score on *Stimulation*—lines B, H, and N give the score on *Handling*, etc.

Scores can vary from 3 to 15. Any score 11 and above is *high;* any score 7 and below is *low*. From the Department of Health, Education and Welfare publication, *Smoker's Self-Testing Kit*, 1975.

To be sure, there can be subtle pressures from one's family. In one typical midwestern case, for instance, a wife was so upset over her husband's puffing away that she forced him to indulge only in the garage. The family's conflict, coupled with humiliation, eventually led this man to the decision that he had to end his addiction, if only to gain control over himself and his own fate. After he stopped smoking, he also reestablished his shaky family balance.

According to a government study of smokers and what they think of themselves, the lack of self-control ranks high. "You are bothered by the knowledge that you cannot control your desire to smoke," explains one psychologist. "Awareness of this challenge to your self-control may make you want to quit." In many cases, the search for self-mastery leads to self-mastery.

The next chapter tells you just how a smoker can move on to the attack and to victory.

6

Stopping by Yourself

The scene is a large, busy hospital. A nurse follows the cardiologist into a patient's room. He had been brought in last night with chest pains. Feeling better now, he is just lighting up when the doctor arrives.

The physician shakes his head. "This ought to be your last cigarette," he says, "if you want to overcome your angina pectoris."

The patient hesitates, then takes another pleasurable puff. He looks at the nurse who stands at the door. Their eyes meet. She understands instantly. Earlier that morning, she had herself been smoking at the nurse's station. The angina victim had seen her through the open door because the desk was directly in his field of vision. Neither of them speak now. She knows what the patient is thinking. *Why shouldn't I smoke when the hospital staff does it?*

But the patient is tactful and considerate. He remains silent. Besides, the cardiologist is examining him.

The nurse decides to restrict her little self-indulgence to the cafeteria. For one thing, she had sneaked the smokes while on duty, a forbidden act. For another thing, the smell of tobacco on her breath and uniform may have influenced the coronary care patient to light up.

The nurse's lunch break comes up in an hour. She decides that she can wait that long for her Virginia Slims.

Without realizing it, this thirty-five-year-old woman is on her way to becoming a nonsmoker. Unconsciously, she employs the psychological technique of "small beginnings."

Some psychologists recommend it. Munich's Dr. Brengelmann, in a long study on behalf of the German government's public health authorities, came to the same conclusion. He writes:

"If the proposed target is too ambitious to permit an optimally high frequency of reinforcement, it must be broken up into smaller units."

It's true: You need to start somewhere: You can begin by delaying your smokes. You can intentionally start to cut down—a measure that is also known as "tapering off."

No two people are alike, but in some cases, the cutting-down process can wean you away from the two-packs-a-day addiction.

"Small Beginnings" includes the acknowledgement that you *may* be addicted, that you may have a problem, and that you earnestly want to begin to search for solutions. Never mind that the latter may be just stopgap measures; they are a start. Mark Twain, who was a heavy smoker himself, explained it well enough: "Habit is habit, and not to be flung out the window by any man, but coaxed downstairs a step at a time."

In the same sense, at least one physician, Dr. A.G. Christen, has observed that the forthcoming habit-change is not necessarily "an all-or-nothing proposition." According to this expert, smokers fail to understand the significance of the "dose response" relationship: The less one smokes, the less the hazard. The smoker who has gone from three or four packs a day to one pack a day should realize that he or she has made great strides. Many people appear to quit in graduated fashion over a prolonged period.

The main point is to understand the need for change, and acceptance of possible failure.

Rationalizations for Smoking

Naturally, it all depends on what type of smoker you are. In what must be the most exhaustive and best-defined study, U.S. government researchers found that the reasons for smoking varied a great deal, but smokers could be placed in general categories.

The pleasure seeker truly enjoys cigarettes, especially after meals, or with liquor. According to the studies, this "positive smoker" can often be helped. When I was battling cigarettes many years ago, a woman friend seriously suggested that if I wanted to light up, she'd make love with me instead. As often as I wished. Not a bad idea!

The I-need-cigarettes-to-cope type, also known as the "negative smoker" reaches for his or her pack when life gets too tense, too stressful, too problematic, which may be thirty times a day. Such people may be able to quit if they can also change their hectic, anxious life patterns. Support from a loved one, counselling, or both, will make things easier.

The Habitual Smoker may develop almost Pavlovian reflexes: He or she must indulge with a cup of coffee, a glass of beer, the incoming mail, an outgoing telephone call and many other situations. Dr. Jerome Schwartz, a California-based government expert, suggests that such individuals need to develop "barriers" such as "forgetting" matches, wrapping cigarette packages into plastic and sealing them with rubber bands.

Stimulation Smokers need a cigarette to wake them up. It also seems to help organize energies during the day. Sometimes they smoke to keep themselves going. This type finds it easier to quit if he or she uses safe substitutes to achieve the same effect: a brisk walk, deep-breathing exercises, etc.

Motivation and Impetus

All these initial efforts are made easier if you have a clear-cut motivation to cut down or quit altogether. We have already seen in the previous chapter that for some people, including this writer, a better athletic performance can drive us to that quitting threshold.

Dr. J.C. Brengelmann, a well-known authority of the Max Planck Institute in Munich, West Germany, checked into the motivations of some 400 ex-smokers. In more than 65 percent of the cases "fear of illness" or "actual illness" were the decisive factors. In this respect it might be of value to reread Chapter 4 of this book. Smoking causes more than six times as many deaths as car accidents! Remind yourself about the ultimate fates of certain movie idols—like Humphrey Bogart, for instance. Or ask about the famous broadcasters such as Edward R. Murrow. Cigarette-related cancer killed both of them. Clark Gable, a heavy smoker, died of a heart attack.

An acquaintance of mine, a heavy Pall Mall consumer, immediately quit after his wife died of throat cancer. Quite often, those High Priests of modern society, the physicians, will bear down hard on a person and bring about a change. In one typical case, a stomach ulcer-plagued man visited his city's leading specialist.

The conversation between them:

Doctor: Do you smoke?

Patient: Yes, I do.

Doctor: Then I won't see you today. You can come back after you've quit.

Likewise, a well-known surgeon, who is much in demand in a large western metropolis, asks patients: "When did you smoke your last cigarette?"

"About an hour ago . . ."

"Well, that was the very last one in your life. This is it." Many patients are so intimidated by The Great Doctor's command that they never touch another.

For many women, pregnancy often brings that moment of truth and the true motivation. A future mother often realizes that she has no right to endanger the health of her unborn child. Later, just before delivery, oxygen is needed in the blood. And afterward, if she nurses her baby, she will surely want to keep nicotine out of her mother's milk.

There are also many people who quit, or cut down, for the sake of loved ones: a father who sees his youngsters' or wife's worried faces, or hears the blunt question "Will you do it for my sake?" A man of my acquaintance, a chain smoker, jettisoned his addiction because his fiancee, whom he adored and would have lost, had strong feelings about self-pollution. And a severely addicted writer made the crucial habit change as "a memorial" to her dying mother.

The will to live remains the strongest motivator. Dr. Isaac Rosenfeld, of Cornell University, smoked until one day about fifteen years ago. He was demonstrating a new radioelectrocardiograph at a scientific meeting. "I was wearing the device, walking about a large auditorium, smoking—and transmitting my electrocardiogram to an oscilloscope several hundred yards away. Some doctors looking at the screen noticed irregularities of the heart rhythm. When they asked the technician who the subject was, she pointed to me. I came back to the oscilloscope and to my dismay saw on the screen my electrocardiogram with several 'extra beats', increasing in number every time I inhaled the cigarette smoke. I had been totally unaware of them."

Like 100,000 other U.S. physicians, Dr. Rosenfeld quit.

For many people, the right moment comes when they have a cold. Barbara Walters, the TV personality, once explained that she became a nonsmoker that way. In other instances, the awareness that you have lost your sense of smell or begun to deaden your delicate tastebuds can propel you toward a decision.

All the cessation experts agree that you need to *list* the reasons why you want to cut down or quit.

This should be done in writing.

For instance:
- I can save money if I stop. Right now I'm spending $600 a year on the habit. The $600 could be spent on a better vacation.

Or:
- I'll get along better at the office. My co-workers don't smoke, and they've begun to resent the clouds I send across to their desks.

Or:
- I'm approaching age fifty next week. I want to make the most of the rest of my life.

The list should be consulted every night before you go to bed, or in the morning before you get up.

Tapering Off

The scientists tell us that there are basically two ways to quit smoking cigarettes.

You stop abruptly and completely. This sudden method is known as "Cold Turkey." It means that you're through. Period. Not even one more cigarette.

Or, you can try to taper off as a stepping stone to total abstention.

A researcher for the U.S. Public Health Service has found that many smokers consider the prospect of giving up cigarettes altogether "a little short of terrifying." Health authorities, therefore, stress the importance of reduction with the hope that it may ultimately lead to completely breaking the habit. Speaking at the World Conference on Smoking and Health, Godfrey M. Hockbaum of the U.S. Public Health Service urged this approach:

> Perhaps we should, in our appeals, not insist, as so many of us are inclined to do, that the only alternative to cancer and emphysema, is total abstinence. Perhaps we should present complete abstinence as the single most desirable alternative. . .but allow that any substantial decrease in cigarette consumption is better than nothing. It is very likely that thousands of smokers, who continue to smoke with both fear and a feeling of futility, may try to do at least something.

In their many years of studying the problem the U.S. Public Health Service and researchers from the National Cancer Institute compiled a list of do's and don'ts for individuals who want to cut down:

Smoke only half of each cigarette.

Each day, postpone lighting your first cigarette by one hour.

Decide you will smoke only during odd or even hours of the day.

Decide beforehand how many cigarettes you'll smoke during the day.

For each additional smoke, give a dollar to your favorite charity.

Don't smoke when you first experience a craving. Wait several minutes; and, during this time, change your activity or talk to someone.

Stop buying cigarettes by the carton. Wait until one pack is empty before buying another.

Stop carrying cigarettes with you at home and at work. Make it difficult to have one.

Smoke only under circumstances that are not especially pleasurable for you. If you like to smoke with others, smoke alone.

Make yourself aware of each cigarette by using the opposite hand, or putting cigarettes in an unfamiliar location or different pocket to break the automatic reach.

If you light up many times during the day without even thinking about it, try to look in a mirror each time you put a match to your cigarette— you may decide you don't need it.

Don't smoke "automatically." Smoke only those cigarettes you really want.

Switch to a brand you find distasteful.

Change your eating habits to aid in cutting down. For example, drink milk, which is frequently considered incompatible with smoking. End meals or snacks with something that won't lead to a cigarette.

Don't empty your ashtrays. This will not only remind you of how many cigarettes you have smoked each day, the sight and smell of stale butts will be very unpleasant.

The tapering-off method need not be cut-and-dried. It can vary. Actor Tony Curtis, for instance, devised his own cutting-down plan. He had been a heavy consumer for two decades when he decided to count his daily smokes. After a month's averaging, he knew that he was on about thirty cigarettes a day. Tony Curtis told an audience the next step: "That's when I realized that 30 was the habit I had to break myself of," he said. "After the first month, I started to cut back." He cut back from thirty to twenty-seven a day about four weeks before he was due to quit, then to fifteen a day about three weeks before the last day. "When I got down to the last week, I was down to five a day and that's when I realized that smoking had become an imposition and I eliminated cigarettes from my psyche. It's been 20 years since I stopped smoking and never once have I wanted another cigarette."

He didn't find it too hard to stop. And the graduated system helped ease the "withdrawal symptoms."

A number of excellent self-help plans have been devised for individuals who want to cut down (see Bibliography). All of these plans recommend *that you keep track of every cigarette you smoke in writing*. List the activity that prompted you to reach for your little treat ("with coffee," "pre-work tension," "opening mail" or whatever). Put down the time of each smoke, and on each day's sheet, record the number of cigarettes consumed. The latter will be your clue to see if you are really tapering off.

Such bookkeeping has a dual purpose. It also identifies your reason for each indulgence. There are some good books and booklets available that will help you keep track; one of the good methods is a "Smokechart" for your recordkeeping. (See Bibliography.) Experts suggest that a heavy smoker taper off to a level of twelve to fourteen cigarettes a day, never more or less.

The light smoker should taper off proportionately, i.e., from twelve cigarettes to three a day. Health workers insist that light smokers—if they can stick to ten or fewer cigarettes a day—suffer fewer ill effects from their indulgence than heavy smokers do from theirs. On the other hand, light smokers often sink deeper into an addiction; stress can cause them to increase how much they smoke very quickly.

Going Cold Turkey

Certain cessation experts favor the tapering-off system; they feel that you are "gradually detoxifying" yourself, which is easier than the brutal "cold turkey" break.

Not everyone agrees.

B.F. Skinner, a well-known psychologist, claims that it is harder to break a habit slowly. "Compare it to *slowly* cutting off the tail of a dog. It's easier to cut it off completely," says Dr. Skinner. For the true addict the slow withdrawal may thus become extremely difficult. Such a person must go the abrupt route.

In either case, you will have to overcome certain obstacles. And whether you only smoke twenty cigarettes a day, like many people, or two packs, you will need to gather your inner forces against the nicotine addiction.

All of which boils down to the fact that you must want to stop. *You decide to do it.*

Half-hearted or impulsive-angry attempts just won't do. The attack has to be well-planned and executed. You are in good company: according to one government survey, since 1964 at least 94 percent of more than 40 million smokers have quit on their own. Many of them have used the Cold Turkey system.

Two UCLA researchers have concluded that in most cases, the method works better than gradual withdrawal. It is especially effective for the heavily addicted person. Many well-established clinics (like the 5-Day Plan, for instance) are totally in favor of total, sudden quitting. This eliminates the scourge of one tapering off problem: in a crisis you won't be tempted to slide back into your old smoking levels. In most cases, you can stay off altogether.

On the other hand, the Cold Turkey method demands more of a commitment. You cannot be wishy-washy about it. You cannot procrastinate. Unnecessary delays can be avoided. Just pick a day. The American Cancer Society has a good name for it—"Q"-Day.

Quitting Day

The choice is yours, of course: the "Day" can be three months away, or only one week down the pike. But the "Day" needs to be engraved in your calendar and in your mind. Indelibly.

"Q-Day": March 15th.

The date needs to be selected carefully. It should not be the next day. The true smoker deserves some mental preparation. You have to get ready for this milestone in your life.

Don't pick a tense period at work, or the week of a pending divorce. Avoid stressors of any kind. No crucial business meetings, exams, deadlines.

A vacation is always a good time because you can concentrate on quitting. A well-known author decided that his best "Q"-Day would be the first day of a cruise. And indeed, as he walked up the gangplank of the "Island Princess," also known as the "Love Boat," the author tossed his last cigarette pack into the dirty waters below. His quitting day had been perfectly selected.

Jackie Rogers, founder of SmokEnders, a well-known personality in the cessation field, chose her wedding anniversary as the cut-off date.

The Rogers family planned a ski vacation in Vermont to celebrate. Jackie remembers that "what used to be an agony of a drive was so nice: It was a long trip, and I didn't have to offend Jon by smoking in the car."

A holiday, a weekend, can also be good choices. "Make the date sacred," advises one expert. "Don't let anything change it."

To be sure, there may be weeks (or even months) between your "I-choose-to-quit" decision and the actual "historic" moment.

One Michigan man, for instance, made up his mind in October that he'd smoke his last cigarette on Christmas Eve. And he did.

Many individuals pick New Year's Day or Easter or sometime when they are relaxed. Your birthday offers an excellent possibility; after all, you start a new and hopefully healthy year in your life. The fixed date reinforces your determination.

According to the American Cancer Society's "I Quit Kit," probably the best situation is one in which you would not be too tempted to smoke anyway, say a long hike or a cross-country ski trip. Or on a date with someone important to you who wants you to quit.

What can you do to add a serious note to that all-important day? What kind of reinforcements would help?

First of all, take the advice of the psychology team hired by the American Cancer Society. According to these skilled researchers, "making an announcement makes the difference."

Tell your spouse or closest friend. "On March 15th, I plan to quit smoking."

Inform the people at your office, especially those who are nonsmokers. Let them admire you.

In one of the most dramatic episodes, Willy Brandt, a leading German politician and former mayor of West Berlin, told the German people in an interview: "Next Sunday is my day. *Ich gebe das rauchen auf.* I give up smoking." With an announcement such as this one, on national (and later international) television, there was no way out.

Brandt had to stick to his statement. And he did. In Sweden, a Health Ministry spokesperson advised the public: "Tell your friends about your resolution. This will reinforce your own resolve and also prevent others from offering you a cigarette. And after telling your acquaintances that you're through with cigarettes, you will feel indeed pressured not to start again."

Dr. Art Ulene, a well-known physician and television personality, and a California Station, KABC-TV, also came up with the idea of a "Personal Contract." You can use it to make a commitment to yourself.

The "public statement" to others and the "contract" with yourself can be followed on the actual "Day" by some other proven measures. Among them:

- Throw away all cigarettes and matches. Hide lighters and ashtrays.
- Visit the dentist, and have your teeth cleaned to get rid of tobacco stains. Notice how nice they look, and resolve to keep them that way.

- Make a list of things you would like to buy yourself or someone else. Estimate the cost in terms of packs of cigarettes, and put the money aside to buy these presents.
- Keep very busy on the big day. Go to the movies, exercise, take long walks, go bike riding.
- Buy yourself a treat, or do something special to celebrate.

I, _____ do hereby promise myself that, as of: _____, _____
I shall commit myself to the following course of action (check one):
☐ Remain a nonsmoker forever
☐ Quit smoking completely
☐ Cut back to _____ cigarettes per day

Signature: _____ Date: _____

Witnessed by: _____

How to Achieve Success

Although it was many years ago that I personally quit, I still remember a friend's suggestion. He told me to get hold of some posters from various health groups. (See organizations in Appendix 2.) My friend had done it himself, temporarily plastering his apartment walls with posters that read, "Cancer Cures Smoking!" The British Medical Association was kind enough to send me some magazine-sized photos of worried-looking, lined males faces sprouting lighted cigarettes: "THINK!" read the legend. I glued these "Think" pieces on the wall of my bathroom, where they still hang, many years later.

On "Q"-Day, your "I-choose-not-to" decision can also be strengthened with another ploy. An Illinois student made a bet with a friend. He bet $10 that he could get along without tobacco for two weeks. He won. Making a bet can also work for you.

In another instance, a young Wyoming woman made a wager with her boyfriend. She bet she would quit on such and such a day. If she did, she would buy him a celebration dinner at Cheyenne's best restaurant. And that is precisely what happened.

Naturally, there will be hurdles to overcome. And you need to be somewhat ruthless in leapfrogging over them.

For instance: After deciding to quit, I went to visit a certain physician (an internist) because of a lingering flu. I'd consulted him once before, but the subject of cigarettes had not come up in our conversations. This time, I told him about my "Q"-Day. He was all for it and actually rattled off a series of medical statistics to underline the wisdom of my decision. Yet on my way out, to my utter surprise, I saw the internist standing in the hall. He was talking to a nurse. He puffed away wildly and greedily on a butt. I decided that I would never see him again. Dr. Bryan Brook, an expert on the cessation systems, even suggests to his patients that they need to re-evaluate whom they will date or their choice for a roommate.

It is also helpful to consider yourself a nonsmoker from now on. My first day *sans* cigarettes was backed up by signs I'd ordered for my house. Made of wood, they read, "Thanks for not smoking." The attitude change has to be a total one. A woman I know decided that her house needed repainting. She asked two painting contractors to come and give her an estimate. One of them arrived with a Marlboro clamped between his teeth. She sent him packing before he could even look at the job. In my case, I shunned typists who might scatter ashes in my office or burn holes into manuscript pages. If all this seems callous, so be it.

Consider yourself a pole vaulter; you need to jump over all the hurdles.

One of them is the constant temptation to get hold of a cigarette. Clyde Jones, an Oklahoma-born tennis player (and former three-pack-a-day smoker) says that the first day is the hardest. But Jones split his Cold Turkey morning into thirty-minute segments. "That's really helpful," Jones explains. "After the first half hour, you say to yourself, 'Okay, now another half hour!' And you'll do it." Jones suggests that after one hour, you say, "Okay, now one more hour." And so you get through the first day.

If you have smoked for some time you will miss the tobacco-filled paper between your fingers and the almost automatic movements of your hands. One expert figured out that in a year's time an habitual smoker will actually move the hand to the mouth some 40,000 times.

So what do you do to overcome this problem? A substitute is needed. One famous American TV comic, a heavy smoker, is seen twirling pencils instead. On occasion, he has even broken them. Some physicians swear that orange juice is one of the best substitutes; after all, smokers' bodies are notoriously deprived of vitamin C and can use plenty of it.

One should also remember that cigarettes once gave you some pleasure, or you wouldn't have smoked. Sigmund Freud's famous quote is truly apropos this situation. Here's what the father of psychiatry had to say: "Whoever understands the human mind, knows that hardly anything is harder for a man to give up than a pleasure he has once experienced. Actually, we can never give anything up; we only exchange one thing for another. What appears to be a renunciation is really the formation of a substitute or surrogate."

Be prepared to find a temporary substitute. Lay in a supply of fresh fruit in season, carrot sticks, celery stalks, sugarless chewing gum, nuts or whatever else you might crave. At this point don't worry about gaining weight. Pamper yourself. But, stimulants or strong alcohol are not recommended. Avoid both at least during the first two weeks of cigarette abstention. There is plenty of the research data on this topic. Two examples? At the respected Continental Health Evaluation Center in Boulder, Colorado, and at the famous Pritikin Longevity Center in Santa Monica, California, the stop-smoking experts warn that you ought to stay away from liquor or coffee. Both stimulate your body to crave nicotine once more. Besides, who needs to replace one bad habit with another.

Indeed, some people keep craving it, and then give in to the temptation. Such people are often more successful in breaking their habit by avoiding the solo cessation route.

A group approach may be more effective.

7

Stopping With the Help of a Group

"In union there is strength," says Dr. Florence Rhyn Serlin, a psychologist whose colleagues agree that for some individuals, a group often does wonders. The smokers quit in unison. And while some of them may start up again, others are cured forever.

Why should certain groups do so well? A British researcher, for instance, discovered that one feminist gathering managed to double the quitting chances for the individual women. Reason? The support from other feminists worked like a charm. Indeed, many stop-smoking clinics can achieve a fine cohesion. This writer stopped with the assistance of the well-known 5-Day Plan, for which participants—in this case, about fifty of them—met for five evenings.

Group action is especially successful when the people have one common aim (which is also the basis of Alcoholics Anonymous). Many smoking "cessation" sessions are headed by experts in the field, including physicians, psychologists, social workers, nurses. Naturally such "quit-cigarettes" meetings can pay off only if you faithfully attend all the sessions. This takes discipline. You are expected to pay attention and to follow through afterward.

Moreover, joint action suffuses a person with an extra measure of self-confidence, which not everyone possesses on his or her own. The gathering of prospective quitters need not always be led by a specialist in the field. In one instance, a group of friends got together. They assembled in a quiet Oregon home and set out to discuss their addiction. A nurse furnished some material for study. By reading up on the subject, about 60 percent of the participants managed to go on the nicotine-less wagon. They supported one another through telephone calls and further get-togethers.

There are a tremendous number of stop-smoking programs of all kinds. Some of them are crassly commercial and cost you an arm and a leg. Others have no scientific basis, and still others, while excellent, are unknown to the public.

Just how do you choose a smoking cessation program? And how do you find it?

This chapter will answer the above questions.

As a preliminary, you might profit from the many years of worldwide research by Dr. J.C. Brengelmann of the Max Planck Institute, Munich. Professor Brengelmann compiled some basic questions that help you determine in advance if a group is truly worthwhile. Among his points:

Does the group therapy have a proven record for effectiveness or have most of the participants gone back to their old tobacco ways?

Is the program practical enough to interest most people? For instance, will you receive enough helpful pointers to get results? Will the length of the program fit into your plans? And lastly, is the clinic financially affordable?

Can the program be made easily available to you? Not everyone could take part in a distant cessation clinic. Dr. Brengelmann also makes it his point to state, "The lack of availability generally precludes the use of a psychiatrist. There just are not enough psychiatrists to go around."

In an additional study, on behalf of Germany's Federal Center for Health Education, Brengelmann suggests that the group should have a proven record of at least "a relative permanence, with reliable data about relapses..." Likewise, the dropout rate during the sessions is an important indicator of the success of a program. It cannot be much good if people lose interest. Also, there should always be a "maintenance" or "follow-up" phase to check on how you are doing.

In my own research, I have also found that you need to distrust any organization that charges you almost as much per get-together as a private hour with a psychiatrist. Certain commercial enterprises spend too much on advertising; they naturally try to recoup these expenditures from you. Dr. Jerome Schwartz, one of America's leading experts in the health care field, suggests that you take a close look at the financial outlay: What is the total program cost? Are there extras you would want? What is the additional cost?

Is a deposit required? Are refunds offered?

Is the balance due upon admission, or over a period of time?

How many sessions are involved? How many total hours?

Nonprofit clinics are recommended for those who want to be helped without spending hundreds of dollars. The most expensive of all programs are the live-in clinics at some excellent hospitals.

Any clinic may work. Or it may not. In the final analysis, only the individual can achieve success.

The 5-Day Plan

One of the most popular group approaches in the world, the "5-Day Plan," is offered at the many Seventh-Day Adventist Hospitals in North America and at some medical centers in Europe.

The participants register on a volunteer basis, usually after learning about the "Plan" from announcements in local newspapers, radio broadcasts, posters, physician's offices and so on.

A modest registration fee is charged to defray the cost of the materials. Why should the 5-Day Plan be so much less expensive than most others? For one thing, its organizers do not have to rent convention and conference rooms at large hotels. They use cooperating hospital auditoriums instead.

Created by a physician and a pastor in 1959, the 5-Day Plan is not run by profiteers, but by dedicated, motivated health workers—M.D.s and advisors—who volunteer their services. Up to now, about 30 million persons have used this nonprofit cessation method.

This crash-course requires five consecutive evenings of ninety-minute sessions, with several weekly follow-up meetings thereafter. Thanks to a set of standard materials and procedures, the general content of the clinics is relatively uniform all over the world. Most course leaders stick closely to the proven content of the program—especially the manual—while films and other illustrative material may vary.

Indeed, what can you expect during your sessions? They usually include:

- Lectures or discussions by a health educator-physician team on the physiological, as well as psychological, aspects of the smoking problem. Several medical doctors are on hand during the five evenings, as well as a dentist and a nutritionist.
- Films produced by the Cancer Society, Heart Association and Lung Association on smoking and its harmful effects on body and mind.
- Demonstrations of procedures helpful to overcoming the smoking habit.
- An exchange of experiences by participants as they fight the habit under the 5-Day Plan.

Originated by Rev. Elman J. Falkenberg and J. Wayne McFarland, M.D., a clergyman and a physician, the Plan offers a practical approach to personal habit control and suggests sensible health procedures. Groups consist of twenty to eighty persons. And, unlike many of its competitors, the 5-Day Plan believes in the "Cold Turkey" method.

You hand over your cigarettes on the first night. Dr. McFarland explains: "We feel that the best way to quit smoking is to stop all at once—none of this tapering-off business. The reason: It is better to have a few rough days and be through with it than to drag it out for weeks and months. You can make a clean sweep of this thing and do it easier than you think. It is our purpose to help you get over the craving as rapidly as possible—in fact, in five days' time."

Fortunately, the lectures and demonstrations are backed by practical advice dealing with the withdrawal symptoms. You are taught to breathe deeply, for instance, whenever the urge to smoke strikes. You inhale deeply and exhale completely. This brings large quantities of oxygen into the body and thus helps calm your smoker's nerves.

The 5-Day Plan organizers also recommend that you drink six to eight glasses of water and eat lots of fresh fruit during those crucial first twenty-four hours. You are encouraged to treat yourself to goodies like fresh berries, fresh pineapple, bananas, grapes. You learn to stay away from spicy meals or coffee; these make people want to smoke. Because cigarettes are often considered a "reward," the Plan teaches that you can substitute something else for the weed. Orange juice, for example. Every time you thirst for a cigarette, you drink a glass of juice instead. And why not? Pure orange juice is healthy, and it replenishes the nicotine addict's depleted vitamin C. While vitamin C will not kill the urge to smoke, it may promote the smoker's health, which has been under siege from many poisons.

The author of this book was impressed by the 5-Day Plan's companion system: you exchange phone numbers with other people. Using the "partner" (or "buddy") system, you call other would-be quitters during the first, often difficult days. As a result of the practical approach, group action and a well-honed, proven program, quitting statistics are high. After one year, as many as 90 percent of the participants have gained independence from tobacco.

Don't be misled. Sometimes the success rate at the 5-Day seminars is only 50 percent of the participants. However, even this is a significant proportion when you compare it to other programs.

When I participated in the 5-Day Plan more than a decade ago, one of the salient features was the projection of sheer fear. I'll never forget the lung cancer operation on the 5-Day Plan's movie screen, for instance. Since those days, the Plan uses less macabre films, and more "positive reinforcement." The slogan, "I choose not to smoke" has been kept up and the 5-Day Plan still emphasizes instruction. Each ninety-minute session includes excellent slide presentations, lectures, "managing stress" seminars, group exercises and access to books and other free materials. The Plan gives people psychological insight into their addiction and plenty of group support. You can also learn a lot about combating the urge to smoke again.

In some of the clinics, the directors suggest that you rub yourself hard with a cold washcloth. They call this the "Cold Mitten Friction." It stimulates your circulation and so gets you going in the morning. Among numerous celebrities, actor Kirk Douglas and singer-entertainer Johnny Cash took the program. The two entertainers highly recommend the program. In fact, Johnny Cash has written a glowing testimonial.

The St. Helena Hospital Program

The 5-Day Plan is available at many hospitals on an outpatient basis (see following list); in addition, for a wealthier clientele there is the inpatient program at the St. Helena Hospital and Health Center, an accredited, 208-bed medical complex, owned and operated by the Seventh-Day Adventist Church. It is located seventy miles northeast of San Francisco in the mountains at the upper end of Napa Valley. The Health Center, with its hotel-like facility, dates back to 1968. Utilizing the medical and allied health professionals of the hospital, the staff at the Center offers an inpatient adaptation of the outpatient "5-Day Plan."

The participating staff consists of an exercise therapist, nurses, a registered dietician, a public health nutritionist, a clinical counselor, a psychologist, registered physical therapists, a health educator and a group of interested community physicians who specialize in thoracic surgery and endoscopy, preventive medicine, physical medicine, cardiology, internal medicine, radiology, neuropsychiatry and family practice.

The inpatient Stop-Smoking Plan consists of a concentrated five-day health education and physical course. The fee amounts to almost $1000, for which you get your private hospital accommodations and buffet-style meals as well. Each day begins at 7 A.M. and ends at 9:30 P.M. You are kept busy throughout the day. In addition to the format of the "5-Day Plan," the hospital staff offers additional testing, daily group therapy sessions directed by a psychologist, physical therapy and tension and weight management courses.

What is a typical St. Helena day like? Here is an outline of activities for the Monday following admission to the program:

6:30 A.M.	Patients are awakened
7:00	Morning exercise
7:45	Breakfast in the dining room
8:15	Understanding spiritual resources, Chapel (optional)
8:30	Film: "Ashes to Ashes"
9:10	Group therapy
10:00	Physical exercise in the gymnasium
10:30	Sauna
11:30	Weight management lecture
12:30 P.M.	Lunch in the dining room
1:30	Tour to Napa Valley points of interest
2:30	Recreational activities in the pool or adjacent areas
3:00	Physical therapy appointment—massage, hotpacks, etc.
4:00	Tennis, Ping-Pong, or crafts, etc.

5:45	Dinner in the dining room
7:00	"Physiology of Exercise"
8:00	"Lung Physiology and Smoking" (includes discussion of pulmonary function study reports)
9:00	Patients retire

And here are the addresses of inpatient 5-Day Plan hospitals.

Florida Hospital
601 E. Rollins Street
Orlando, FL 32803

Washington Adventist Hospital
7600 Carroll Avenue
Takoma Park, MD 20012

Portland Adventist Medical Center
10123 SE Marker Street
Portland, OR 97216

Wildwood Sanitarium and Hospital
Wildwood, GA 30757

St. Helena Hospital & Health Center
Deer Park, CA 94576

Also very helpful are hospitals with Outpatient 5-Day plans. Here is a list of such hospitals in the United States.

Battle Creek Sanitarium & Hospital
197 North Washington Avenue
Battle Creek, MI 49016

New England Memorial Hospital
5 Woodland Road
Stoneham, MA 02180

Castle Memorial Hospital
640 ULUKAHIKI Street
Kailua, HI 96734

Paradise Valley Hospital
2400 East Fourth Street
National City, CA 92050

Feather River Hospital
5974 Pentz Road
Paradise, CA 95969

Porter Memorial Hospital
2525 So. Downing
Denver, CO 80210

Florida Hospital
601 East Rollins Street
Orlando, FL 32803

Portland Adventist Medical Center
10123 Southeast Market Street
Portland, OR 97216

Glendale Adventist Medical Center
1509 Wilson Terrace
Glendale, CA 91206

St. Helena Hospital & Health Center
Deer Park, CA 94576
Offers a live-in-program

Hackettstown Community Hospital
651 Willow Grove Street
Hackettstown, NJ 07840

Simi Valley Adventist Hospital
2975 North Sycamore Drive
Simi Valley, CA 93065

Hinsdale Sanitarium and Hospital
120 North Oak Street
Hinsdale, IL 60521

Tempe Community Hospital
1500 South Mill Avenue
Tempe, AZ 85281

Huguley Memorial Seventh-Day
Adventist
Medical Center
P.O. Box 6337
Fort Worth, TX 76115

Walla Walla General Hospital
933 Bonsella
Walla Walla, WA 99362

Kettering Medical Center
Kettering, OH 45429

Washington Adventist Hospital
Takoma Park, MD 20012

Loma Linda University
Medical Center
Loma Linda, CA 92354

White Memorial Medical Center, Inc.
1720 Brooklyn Avenue
Los Angeles, CA 90033

Madison Hospital
500 Hospital Drive
Madison, TN 37115

SmokEnders

Some large profit-minded corporations also operate group therapy smoking cessation programs.

The biggest and best known: SmokEnders. Started by a chain-smoker-homemaker, Jacquelyn Rogers, and her dentist husband Jon, in 1968, SmokEnders now has chapters and franchises in dozens of North American and several European cities.

It took a good chunk of the Rogers' own savings to start the commercial enterprise. But SmokEnders paid off. Jackie Rogers and her husband became millionaires. The Rogers charge several hundred dollars for eight 2-hour sessions. (How many hundreds of dollars? You can compare the individual cost to a month's apartment rent for two people in a major U.S. metropolitan city.)

The SmokEnders' concept differs considerably from the 5-Day Plan. The latter is nonprofit. SmokEnders aim is frankly monetary.

The 5-Day Plan insists on the Cold Turkey Method.

SmokEnders believes in your continuing to smoke until the fifth week. The company's ads claim that "Cold Turkey is a turkey. It's a nasty, inefficient way to quit. Nasty—because it makes you climb the walls. And inefficient—because it usually doesn't stick. SmokEnders takes a more intelligent approach. We reasoned, that if people can learn how to smoke, they can learn how not to smoke. It works. It's not cold turkey. More like warm chicken."

The "5-Day Plan" doesn't compromise. By contrast, SmokEnders coddles you. Comfort is the key. No great demands at first. No embarrassment. In the initial meeting, the speaker emphasizes that "this is not 'a will-power program'." Instead, attitudes about smoking are "retrained." Smokers do not "give up" cigarettes, they *"get rid of"* them. The meetings help you practice that riddance. "You taught yourself to smoke—you can teach yourself how not to smoke." In short, the group programs rely on behavior modification.

Seminars are always taught by SmokEnder graduates, i.e., former smokers. This is a good idea; after all, a former chain-smoker understands what the participant goes through. However, none of the leaders are in the medical profession. The company frankly admits that it is in "the motivation business," but without the "fear tactics" of some other groups. No horror movies or death statistics.

Jacquelyn Rogers: "We *do not threaten* you with death, doom or disaster. We *do not surround* you with portraits of disease and illness. We *do not insult* your intelligence or pressure you with medical visuals that assault you with ravaged lungs and mangled hearts.

"We want to make your SmokEnders experience one of personal growth, insight and understanding—a productive and happy experience."

In brief, SmokEnders pursues the positive approach. Nonsmoking is represented as beautiful. And as motivators, the leaders insist that you *can* stop. "Nonsmoking is reprogramming."

In the first session, the smoker is made to feel welcome via a printed poster on a lectern. It reads, "Relax, Smile and Light Up!"

The introduction is mindful of the Alcoholics Anonymous approach. Your leader—a woman conducted the seminar I attended—explains how she started smoking and how cigarettes came to control her life; how she came to realize how much her life was controlled by them; and how she tried to quit in every way known. Unfortunately nothing worked. Until she tried the SmokEnders plan, that is. The latter is made to appear easy, and indeed, at first you can keep smoking "because smokers need to learn a lot before they can quit successfully." During the sixth, seventh and eighth meetings participants share fears, hopes, tips, experiences. The meetings take place once a week. Each meeting is in two parts: first, smoking attitudes and your personal relationship with the habit are dissected; then, in part two, you learn about the activities that will help you train yourself away from smoking.

"Cut-off" comes at the fifth week and is followed by four more reenforcement meetings.

SmokEnder sessions take place at hotels, motels, churches, schools, department stores and other community centers. SmokEnders also operates a hugely successful "corporate program" for Blue Chip companies in every field, all over the country. At one point, during Secretary Joseph Califano's regime, the clinic was even offered to employees of the Department of Health, Education and Welfare in Washington, D.C.

SmokEnders spends huge amounts of money on advertising. A campaign may cost as much as $1 million. The ads hit hard. One headline promises that, "You will stop smoking on June 2nd!"

The customers are attracted by mass invitations to frequent "Free Introductory Seminars." The rationale for your spending good money is given in SmokEnders' literature: "At our inception, we made the decision to rely on the participant for financing because the tuition payment assures a higher level of commitment than if there were no charge, and clinical evidence reveals that greater commitment yields greater success."

Jacquelyn Rogers also reasons, perhaps correctly, that someone who takes her group program and succeeds, saves enough money on cigarettes to afford this expensive cessation method. In the meantime, a number of celebrities have relied on SmokEnders, among them a much-quoted Joseph Califano, actor Leonard Nimoy, singer Barry Manilow, actress Rosemary Harris, skater Dick Button. All appear in the firm's publicity material.

For more information, just watch your large metropolitan newspaper for the frequent ads. Or write to SmokEnders at 3708 Mt. Diablo Boulevard, Lafayette, CA 94549 or 37 North 3rd Street, Easton, PA 18042.

The American Health Foundation Smoke Cessation System

This highly structured, more reasonably priced course takes five days. After an introductory session, you learn to abstain permanently from smoking via lectures, demonstrations, practice sessions, relaxation training, behavioral rehearsal, eating management, thought-stopping and deconditioning. Participants study the smoking habit from psychological, social, physiological and behavioral viewpoints. The program is based on the philosophy that quitting smoking is easier when you know how to do so. Participants learn to prevent cigarette urge sensations from occurring and to eliminate urge sensations when they do develop.

Participants also receive a packet of stop-smoking booklets that detail the program's techniques and concepts. These include:

Mental imagery and deep breathing exercises designed to decrease anxiety.

Coping skills that enable you to develop a more positive attitude about the quitting process.

Stimulus control—Modifying the environment to eliminate smoking "trigger mechanisms."

Self-reward—Pairing positive reinforcements with the self-rewards.

The American Health Foundation teaches some practical stuff, too. For instance, to increase physical activity instead of smoking. And to "scramble" your daily schedule. For example, take a walk instead of a coffee break during which you might be tempted to smoke. The AHF program costs $150 at this writing.

This enterprise is run by Dr. E.L. Wynder. The AHF address: 320 E. 43rd Street, New York, NY 10017 and AHF, c/o Mahoney Institute, Box 719, Garden City, NY 11530.

American Cancer Society

The ACS features well-established group therapy sessions in many communities. The gatherings number from about eight persons to no more than twenty and are led by physicians, psychiatrists (when available) and ex-smokers, all on a volunteer basis. Strictly nonprofit, the ACS asks only for a small contribution for which you get substantial help, i.e., two hours twice a week for four weeks.

The American Cancer Society operates in some 1000 to 1500 cities and towns on a continuing or on-demand basis. You should call your local American Cancer Society office for information about time and place.

Like the 5-Day Plan, an ACS "buddy" system insures support, and like SmokEnders, the American Cancer Society doesn't insist on immediate jettisoning of a longtime habit. Another advantage is its cost. An individual in modest financial circumstances would be wise to try the ACS program before enlisting with SmokEnders.

The ACS also relies on "positive reinforcement" and on group discussions. After the final meeting, participants are encouraged to support each other in an I.Q. (I Quit) club.

Because of the low costs and the trustworthiness of the ACS, thousands of people get help from them each year; they meet in hospitals, clinics, banks, churches. In some areas, ACS facilitators also work with employees of large companies. Depending on local conditions, chapters of the American Heart Association and the American Lung Association also offer group therapy. The ALA clinics require ninety minutes twice a month and go on for an indefinite period of time.

For additional groups in the U.S. or Canada, you might ask your telephone information service for possible listings for a County Medical Society, County Health Department, State Inter-Agency Council on Smoking and Health, or a Community Hospital, any of which might have cessation programs.

Other programs are listed in the Yellow Pages of your telephone directory under "Smokers Information and Treatment Centers."

8

The Uses of Behavior Therapy and Hypnosis

For many years now, psychologists have focused on the tobacco addiction problem. They have descended *en masse* on cigarette fiends and talked to them individually as well. Clinical psychologists have concentrated on smokers in the manner of botanists taking plants apart. Doctoral theses, reams of reports, entire textbooks have dissected the nicotine affliction from every psychological viewpoint. And of course, these studied scientists devised methods that, if you really want to, help you toss off the habit once and for all.

But what is the most fascinating part about the writings and theories of all these learned men and women?

By and large, they are all saying the same thing.

In general, they suggest that you must take the same one, two, three steps to rid yourself of the cigarette. To be sure, these assorted psychologists all use their own language, and couch their theories in their own varying presentations. But the more that things change, the more they remain the same.

Dr. Johannes Brengelmann, the leading German cessation expert, offers one of the most interesting presentations. He sums up the three stages of behavior triggers and responses for certain smokers:

| Trigger: | Just had a meal; ordered coffee; friend offers a cigarette. | Action: | Begins to smoke: cigarette is lit. |

Results:	Cigarette tastes good, the smoke is fragrant.	Action:	Smoker relaxes.
Responses:	A. Spouse says you are stinking up the house.	Action:	Stub out cigarette.
	B. Friend says your cigarette smells wonderful.	Action:	Light another cigarette.

So much for analysis. Now how about the treatment? Dr. Brengelmann says that we can try to bring the trigger under control before the act of smoking begins. In each case we can change the situation so that it no longer has the same stimulating force (situation control—stimulus control).

We can try to make the feelings accompanying smoking disagreeable (aversion), and finally, we can alter the consequences, for example, by rewarding nonsmoking or penalizing smoking.

The Secrets of Behavior Modification

What does it all amount to? According to Dr. Bryan Brook, a nationally known expert, the profession believes in behavior modification. Explains Dr. Brook, "Behavior modification is an elegant term that's been coined by behavioral scientists *to describe a systematic approach to changing someone.*"

Like Dr. Brengelmann, his colleague in Germany, and psychologists everywhere else, Dr. Brook helps smokers identify their patterns: How did you get started? When do you smoke? What do you get out of it? What would be missing from your life if you stopped smoking? Those questions help the person get some conscious control. Don't forget, smoking becomes unconscious, that's what we mean by "habit." People reach for a cigarette to relax, or calm themselves, or just to be part of the group. Smoking disappears into the subconscious level. A psychologist therefore tries to raise that awareness to a consciousness. This way the "patient" realizes that every time he or she gets nervous, or every time he or she receives criticism, the smoker reaches for a cigarette. Dr. Brook explains: "I try to make a smoker more aware of what started this behavior to begin with, what triggers it now, and what can be substituted for it."

Dr. Brook also points out one important tenet of behavior modification: Therapists don't modify behavior. They just aim to help people modify their own behavior. And in summing up, this psychologist speaks for others when he theorizes that smokers need genuine motivation to break their denial that the habit is harmful; to make the subconscious aspects conscious; and a peer group support.

The latter may be a crucial factor; after all, groups are sometimes led by ex-smokers who have chucked the habit. "If he or she can do it, I can do it," often works as a motivator.

Many psychologists prefer to see patients as a group. Dr. Paul Hansen, of the Continental Health Evaluation Center in Boulder, states that a "person's desired change in behavior is enhanced by a group setting with other smokers." Like all his peers, Dr. Hansen believes that the "support system within the group" is valuable. Moreover, within the support group certain agreements and contracts are made that will assist the person in his or her smoke-ending process. These may include such things as: not getting together immediately following a meal to smoke, not smoking in their rooms, not loaning cigarettes to one another; and agreeing to be supportive in their efforts to stop smoking.

Some Good Counsel From Behavioral Therapists

While the basic ABCs are the same with any number of psychologists in the Behavior Therapy field, some of them have gathered a few practical behavior modification exercises as well.

Make sure that you begin to see smokers in a different light. They are neither chic nor macho nor sophisticated. See them for what they really are: people who cough a lot, have yellow fingers and bad breath. And bear in mind that the greater a person's professional prestige, the bigger the income and education, the more likely he or she is a nonsmoker.

List several reasons for giving up smoking that are intensely personal, that have meaning only for you. Put them down on a piece of paper. Build motivation. From your list of reasons for giving up smoking, select the most important reason; that is, the one that will turn you on and keep you moving. Write it down.

Thought stopping was developed by psychologists to help eliminate obsessive/compulsive thoughts. It works well for thoughts about cigarettes, too. Whenever they occur, yell out the word STOP!!! as loud as you can. This will startle the thought away. Practice this technique at least ten times. There is also a silent version of thought stopping. For this technique, imagine yelling "STOP!!!" while trying to visualize the word in large capital letters, a flashing red light or a STOP sign.

Observe a smoker in a detached way. See how he or she sticks that little white tube into his or her mouth. How silly it looks! Presently the person searches for a match and tries to strike it. It is windy and the match doesn't light. You watch the smoker cup the hands, lean the head away from the wind, try again. Finally, the person is smoking. The whole maneuver seems so useless. So wasteful. Why would anyone draw burning tobacco into their lungs? Why? How superfluous! How unnecessary!

Say to yourself, "I've quit the habit. At last I'll be able to save a few bucks a week. Thank goodness I no longer smoke. I don't want to. I've quit the habit, and I've never felt better in my whole life."

Every day, every half day, every hour, every fifteen minutes, if need be, say these phrases over to yourself. Let them fill your mind.

You program your thinking apparatus along these lines and instruct your subconscious of your decision. As you feed in these positive thoughts day in and day out, the final conscious printout will be along similar lines.

Reward yourself with little things that make you feel good. Treat yourself to a bubble bath; buy the hardcover edition of a book rather than wait for the paperback to come out; get the game or puzzle you have been wanting; buy or pick a flower; picnic in the park during lunchtime; try a new perfume or cologne; give yourself some "me-time."

Hypnosis: Pros and Cons

The patient—a heavy-set man in his late fifties—stretches out in one of those expensive reclining chairs, a sumptuous one, covered with what appears to be leather. The subject has been asked to remove his tie and unbutton the top of his white shirt. The chair is in position, tilted back, almost horizontal.

"How are you feeling?" asks the hypnotist. "Comfortable?"

"Sure am," says the man, visibly relaxing in the $600 recliner chair.

The hypnotist is a woman with an M.A. in Communication, who has also studied at a Clinical Hypnosis School in an eastern metropolis.

The heavy-set man inquires if he can light a cigarette. She shakes her head slightly. He gives up and they have a brief conversation. He says he is a hard-pressed sales manager for a national company. There are too many deadlines, too many quotas, too many problems. So he smokes sixty cigarettes a day to calm himself. Strong cigarettes. Camels. No filters. His doctor has told him about some of the possible medical consequences and suggested he try clinical hypnosis. "It has become respectable," his physician said.

The woman hypnotherapist sits behind the desk, listening intently to her patient.

They discuss his case for awhile, especially his motivations, and whether he has truly decided to quit. He has. And he is ready for hypnosis.

Her voice is very quiet, almost drowsy.

The process begins with complete body relaxation: Comfortable, deep and regular breaths, eyes closed. "Relax your feet, then, your ankles. Now your lower legs, upper legs. Let your muscles relax. Continue breathing deeply.

"Good. Now we're going to let all the muscles in your feet go limp, just let all the tension go."

The sales manager concentrates well.

It takes about ten minutes to put him into a satisfactory trance. He is not asleep. He can move his limbs. He can hear what the hypnotherapist has to say. She drones on softly about what might happen if he continued to smoke.

His high cholesterol levels and high blood pressure, combined with sixty Camels a day, might eventually cause a heart attack. Not tomorrow. Just eventually. He may survive the first attack. But it could be painful. "Oh, yes," the man whispers. "Right there in the chest." And later, she explains, if the pain didn't go away through medication, there might come open heart bypass surgery. "We'll talk about that next time."

Being in a trance means being open to suggestions, such as:

Cigarettes are dangerous to your health.

Among the 18,000 or so hypnotists in the United States, the approach to smoking cessation varies. Dr. William Nemon, a well-known expert, whispers to his patients: "Tobacco is poison to your body . . . you need your body to live . . . you can't allow more poisoning of your body." Dr. Herbert Spiegel, a psychiatrist, a prominent east coast leader in the field, puts you into a mild trance, then says, "I need my body to live. I owe my body this respect . . ." Lester Palmer, a Colorado hypnotist, takes the positive approach. "You *enjoy* being a nonsmoker . . . it is much better to be a nonsmoker . . . you have no desire for cigarettes."

Dick Sutphen, one of the most acclaimed west coast practitioners, takes a positive approach. When the patient reaches the suggestible trance, Sutphen tells him or her: "You have the willpower to quit. You're a strong personality. You can throw away the crutch." And later: "You're losing all desire to smoke . . ." And still later: "You're losing all desire to smoke . . ." And still later: "You've eliminated cigarettes . . ."

How much time does such hypnosis take?

The required time varies. Dr. Spiegel is known for his one-hour-per-patient sessions. No more, no less. A clinic in a western city insists on five one-hour stints. Other practitioners fall somewhere in between. Almost all, however, try to teach you self-hypnosis, so that you can later get along without a hypnotherapist. This is much cheaper, of course. Dr. Spiegel, for instance, charges about twice as much per sixty minutes than a session with a psychiatrist. At this writing, the average costs of hypnosis fluctuate between forty and eighty dollars. Dr. Spiegel gets $130.

These costs may be new but hypnosis itself is not. It even began long before Frans Anton Mesmer, the Austrian physician who gave us the word "mesmerize." Hypnosis went on during medieval times, not always for the best purposes, until surgeons finally got hold of the skills during the nineteenth century. The deepest trance was used as anesthesia for operations, an idea that is still being employed by certain skilled dentists.

Hypnosis gained extra respectability when British physicians tested it on some difficult allergy cases during the mid-sixties. According to the *British Medical Journal*, the power of hypnosis-induced suggestibility was proven in an experiment with twelve patients; all of whom had severe allergies. Before hypnosis, they were injected with the very substances that caused them no end of problems. "You are *not* allergic," they were told by the hypnotist. "You have no symptoms at all." Of the twelve patients, eight emerged without symptoms.

Can anyone be hypnotized?

According to authoritative figures, about 80 percent of the North American or European population can be hypnotized. People of excessively low intelligence and retarded individuals make poor subjects. The same goes for the cynical-hostile type. In short, your cooperation is needed. "Hypnosis is a game you play with your own mind," says one specialist. "For hypnosis to work, people must be able to relax and 'go with it'."

Experts also generally agree that the system doesn't work for a young person who is easily distracted. You must be able to pay attention. This has nothing to do with intelligence level. It need not be high, although the most intelligent persons make the best hypnosis patients because they can concentrate. For some individuals, it takes longer to reach a trance-like state. Others can do it within minutes.

Hypnosis has been applied in many ways. Apart from getting you to stop smoking, the system has been used against over-eating, nail-biting, feeling pain, alcoholism and even sexual malfunctions.

Hypnosis as a Science

Dr. Spiegel considers hypnosis a science and calls it "one of the great therapeutic instruments." Nevertheless, a good portion of the general public fears the clinical hypnotist. When a woman was introduced to a reputable New York hypnotherapist by her family physician, she did not dare follow through but wrote the man a letter instead. In it, she expressed some of her anxieties about the treatment by hypnosis.

To her surprise, she shortly received a letter from the hypnotherapist. "My practice is a busy one," he told her. "But I sympathize with your attitude, which is very common among the public at large. I would like to allay your fears by stating some important points about hypnosis:

"1. Hypnotherapists have no connection with stage hypnotists. We use no swinging pendulums or gimmickry.

"2. We do nothing against your will because we need your cooperation at all times. Resistance or testing your will against hypnosis will make the latter ineffective.

"3. You never surrender your person but retain your own judgement at all times.

"4. It is a misconception that you will be unconscious. You will only be in a light trance during which you are still aware of your surroundings. For instance, you can still hear a fire engine or ambulance passing my office, or the ringing of a telephone.

"5. None of our patients ever suffers 'amnesia', which you say you fear. You'll remember exactly what has taken place while you were in hypnosis. Although totally relaxed, you're alert during the entire procedure. And you can be easily awakened afterward."

Actually, the "afterward" is often being criticized by some cessation experts. One of them, from the respected St. Helena Hospital in California, recently attacked hypnosis in a much publicized interview with UPI. The expert advised people "to think twice about hypnosis. Its success rates are not that promising." Even New York's Dr. Herbert Spiegel, the psychiatrist-hypnotist, does not deny that he may be able to help only "one in five smokers."

Most researchers have also come to the conclusion that unless you buy plenty of hypnotic follow-up sessions, you don't stand much of a chance to kick the habit. ("Those who stop smoking via hypnosis might do it in any case," says one critic.) Other researchers call hypnosis one of "the more short-lived treatments." It wears off easily. In one of the best-known studies, by Dr. G. Grayson of San Francisco, the rub was not the patient's initial reaction; of 233 smokers, 180 stopped, *but only for a short period of time*. Twelve months later, just 73 persons (of the original 233) were still off the weed.

In one amusing true life story, a west coast hypnotist suggested that his patient consider his "cigarette a poisonous snake." After the patient came out of the trance, the hypnotist offered him a smoke. The man at first looked surprised. But a moment later, he said brightly, "Sure, I'll smoke that snake!" And he did, too.

Readers who are interested in contacting a clinical hypnotist can check the Yellow Pages of the local telephone book, the Medical Society or nearest Mental Health Center. Also, any hospital in a large city can provide the names of reputable hypnotherapists.

Auto-Hypnosis

Hypnotherapists recommend that after an initial session or two (or five), you continue on your own. This saves time and money, of course. And it can work. One psychologist explains:

> Self-hypnosis, also called 'auto-hypnosis', is a state of heightened suggestibility wherein personal programming can be directed to and accepted by the subconscious mind. The untapped reservoir of intelligence is brought to the surface and almost anything is possible. Individuals can sometimes match the success of professionals in alleviating their own

behavioral problems. Self-hypnosis also reduces stress and promotes a stronger personality. Most people learn how to induce self-hypnosis by first being hypnotized by a professional.

Naturally, as always, you need to change your attitude before hypnosis. You must truly want to stop smoking.

Experts agree that self-hypnosis has great advantages. It allows you to get involved with yourself. You begin to take responsibility for your own actions. You no longer depend on a therapist.

You can employ auto-hypnosis several times a day. Or every time you crave a cigarette. Some clinics suggest at least ten or more daily self-hypnosis sessions. But unlike the preceding one-hour stints with a hypnotist, these self-administered sessions need not last more than one to ten minutes.

The Cassette Method

One of the leaders in the self-hypnosis field is Dick Sutphen, a Malibu, California, hypnotist. Sutphen has given many public demonstrations of hypnosis throughout the world. Via his Valley of the Sun Company (Box 38, Malibu, CA 90264), Sutphen sells self-hypnosis tapes that help you to stop smoking.

He wisely warns you not to use them while driving a car, lest you fall asleep at the wheel. How about the ideal position at home?

Sutphen advises: "Lying down is best unless it causes you to fall into a normal sleep. Avoid using your tapes when you're very tired. The tape will condition your subconscious mind, and you don't want the tape to condition it to fall asleep when you go into an altered state. If you fall asleep two times while in the prone position, continue further sessions by sitting up for a few days."

The California hypnotist's soothing voice addresses you via the cassette. "Feel your body relax...the relaxing power comes into your toes...you're relaxing all your muscles...permeating every cell, relaxing completely, you feel it in the base of your spine..." Eventually, "all the tension is gone...your mind is filled with peace..."

Sutphen uses a metronome, which truly helps you relax; he applies his skills to other problems also, people who are too tense, for instance, or insomniacs. (An avowed marathoner and health freak, Sutphen also sells tapes that will assist you with weight-loss via self-hypnosis.) In his stop-smoking program, he works through positive reinforcement. "You *have* the willpower—you dislike smoking. There—you quit smoking! You'll awaken feeling good—feel the sense of joy and well being!"

9

Aversion Therapy

"Counter-conditioning" is an extension of Pavlov's "conditioned reflex" theory. As everyone knows by now, Pavlov was able to bring about a dog's salivation by means of a bell—a bell that had previously sounded at feeding time. The process can be reversed, of course. For instance: what if someone zapped you with a small electrical shock every time you touched a cigarette? Or imagine, for a moment, a closed telephone booth or a ski lift gondola, with you in it. The therapist asks you to smoke rapidly and hungrily. You may cough more than usual and even get nauseated in the process. Psychologists call this "counter-conditioning," or "aversive conditioning."

After enough electrical jolts—or a sufficient number of bouts in a smoking chamber—you develop an "aversion" to nicotine.

In one of the most unusual studies of counter-conditioning, a San Mateo, California, therapist fired a light rifle fifty times behind a smoker, who reduced his cigarette intake—presto. An extreme remedy, perhaps. But it illustrates aversion technique par excellence.

The Schick Smoking Control Centers

The multimillion-dollar Schick Institute, an offspring of the Schick Safety Razor Company, has carried the aversion theme to its greatest success. What with two dozen Schick Smoking Control Centers scattered around the U.S., and Schick's own hospitals (the latter for the cure of alcoholism), Schick has not only attacked cigarette addiction, but also weight control (in separate programs).

The basic idea here goes back to one's childhood; if you are punished for something you should not do, you may not do it again. The Schick modus operandi is uniform at all the offices: You come in for an interview during which you are still allowed to smoke, but are also expected to keep track of the number of consumed cigarettes. Your counsellor discusses your motivations and the program with you. Schick prefers patients who really want to quit.

Impulse Therapy

You learn about the costs ($650 at this writing) and the time required (a daily hour from Monday through Friday for one week). The basis of the program is electric shock therapy. Never fear: the electrical impulses can be adjusted to the patient's needs; after all, some people have very low pain thresholds.

The electrical "counter-conditioning" sessions take place in a private room, where the ashtrays are purposefully filled with old butts. The ugly sight and stale smell of these tobacco leftovers supposedly help lead to future aversion.

After the first five sessions, the Schick client "graduates" to an eight-week follow-up-program. Its success is based on the unpleasantness of the electrical shocks. "You can't crave something you associate with annoyance," a Schick executive once told the press.

Each clinic's "impulse business" originates from a black box with switches, dials and wires. During your aversion sessions, the contraption jokingly becomes known (among patients) as the "torture box."

You are hooked up to it by means of an armband that doubles as an electrode. As you light up, you feel the first battery-inflicted shock on your forearm. When you put down your cigarette, the electricity ceases. But each new puff is "punished" with renewed electrical charges.

The Schick therapists make it clear that the current does not run through your whole body, only through your forearm. And in any case, the patient (also known as "client") has a say about the strength of the zaps. In fact, the first-time visitor receives a written prospectus on what will happen after having been hooked up with the impulse box.

After you know all about the shocks, the conversation with your therapist will go like this:

Therapist: We'll start from zero and then we'll work up until you tell me when you feel something. You'll be receiving slight electrical signals or impulses on the surface of your arm. I want you to tell me when you feel anything at all. Once you feel a tingling sensation you tell me to increase the impulses until you feel some discomfort, like a light pinch. Remember, you only need a slight annoyance.

Client: I feel a tingling sensation now.

Therapist: Tell me when you start feeling some discomfort.

Client: That's uncomfortable but it doesn't seem to bother me much.

Therapist: How does that feel?

Client: It's more annoying now—uncomfortable.

Therapist: Shall we leave it there or decrease it?

Client: No, that's fine.

Therapist: All right. Start smoking without inhaling, please.

To be sure, the Schick Institute is optimistic about its programs. One publicist explains: "At Schick, the change can occur in a matter of days. After the first session, the client doesn't like the habit as much. After the second, he likes it even less. After the third, he feels neutral. The fourth session produces the attitude, 'I just don't feel like it.' And after the fifth session, he wouldn't think of continuing the habit. Both his conscious mind and subconscious memory have joyfully united to avoid the habit."

The Schick system actually began at the Shadel Hospital in Seattle, Washington, with an alcohol withdrawal program. The idea was conceived by Patrick Frawley, longtime Schick Safety Razor Company chairman. (His company later bought the Shadel hospitals.) Frawley was eventually joined by the founder of a well-known ad agency, a former General, a professor of chemical engineering and by a small team of physicians.

The alcohol addiction program worked well. After some research, Frawley launched Schick's diet control and stop-smoking centers. The latter claim remarkable results. According to Schick's publicity, 95 percent of the participants stop during the first five days. If they don't, their money is refunded; moreover, within the first twelve months any client can repeat the aversion training at no charge.

Schick's medical programs date back to the mid-sixties, since then, some 150,000 persons have plunked down the stiff fee for the impulse therapy. While the system offers plenty of shock value during the initial stages, patients often go back to their tobacco habit later on. Dr. J.L. Schwartz, a longtime government researcher, explains some of the reasons in *U.S. Public Health Reports*: "The methods reviewed are subject to a number of theoretical criticisms. One is that aversive conditioning relies mainly upon the use of punishment as a motivating force and the effects of punishment frequently are not predictable, especially when no ready substitute for the undesired behavior is available. A further objection is that while conditioning aims at the manipulation of behavior, the link between smoking behavior and associated feelings (anxiety, desire for cigarettes) is not thoroughly understood. Whether or not the aversive conditioning of smoking generalizes to the feelings which give rise to it has not been adequately determined."

Dr. Bryan Brook, a psychologist, agrees with this assessment. "In my opinion, the aversion program can only work *on a short-term basis*," he says. "It turns out to be a lucrative business for the therapists."

Another group of researchers, at Germany's Max Planck Institute, found that the electroshock method "fared badly" in comparison with other cessation techniques. Indeed, only 34 percent of the impulse-therapy patients were still off the weed after one month, and a mere 21 percent were still abstinent after three months. All others, writes Dr. Brengelmann, had gone back to their old nicotine habits. As always, the quitters were committed people. In other words, people who might have quit with other methods, too. Below is a list of Schick Smoking Control Centers.

Arizona

        4910 N. 4th St., #14
        Phoenix, AZ 85018

California

        1390 Market Street
        San Francisco, CA 94102

        Schick Laboratories, Inc.
        Headquarters:
        1901 Avenue of the Stars
        Los Angeles, CA 90067

        2917 Fulton Avenue
        Sacramento, CA 95821

        273 S. Lake Avenue
        Pasadena, CA 91101

        2727 Camino Del Rio So.
        San Diego, CA 92108

Florida

        1312 S. E. 17th Street
        So. Harbor Plaza
        Ft. Lauderdale, FL 33316

        12211 S. Dixie Highway
        Miami, FL 33156

Oklahoma

        50 Penn Place, Mezz, FL.
        Oklahoma City, OK 73118

Texas

        3601 Hulen St.
        Ft. Worth, TX 76107

        13020 Preston Rd., #122
        Dallas, TX 75240

West

        4685 S. Highland Drive
        Salt Lake City, UT 84117

        1100 Denny Way
        Seattle, WA 98409

        Sahara Square Shopping Ctr.
        Las Vegas, NV 89104

        1256 Lloyd Center
        Portland, OR 97232

The Rubber-Band Method

Schick's elaborate aversive conditioning often reduces the number of cigarettes you smoke, at least for awhile. An even simpler system is recommended by Dr. D.L. Geisinger, an aversion specialist.

    Dr. Geisinger suggests that you put a one-eighth-inch rubber band around your wrist. Do it when you get up in the morning; make sure it is not too tight or too loose. And then? "Whenever you get besieged by the urge to smoke and want or need additional help in countering this pressure, snap the band against your wrist by stretching it several inches and then letting it go. Alternate snapping it against either the sides or the inner or outer part of the wrist: Keep snapping it until the desire to smoke abates for at least 15 seconds."

The aversion specialist claims that you need to stick to the rubber band technique for a minimum of one month. Three months is better. Should it hurt? Dr. Geisinger has worked it all out to every detail. Specifically, he suggests that the snap of the band is sufficient to cause *some pain*, but not to cut your skin or damage you in any way; is delivered as soon as the nagging impulse to smoke *begins*, and *simultaneously* with it if and when it persists. It should *continue* until the urge leaves for at least fifteen seconds (leaves for any reason—even, for example, because you got distracted when the phone began to ring).

The whole idea sounds intriguing. And compared to Schick or SmokEnders, the price is right.

Aversion Therapy: Rapid Smoking

One "aversion technique" gets you to smoke in a small, hot, closed-in space. The latter can resemble a telephone booth, or look like a ski area gondola. The "chamber" may also be a small airless room, complete with a small window through which the "therapist" watches your "progress." (In one case, wearing a gas mask.) A California psychologist actually constructed a metal lung large enough for one person. The lung did double duty: it reminded the offender what smoking can do to his or her breathing, and it encapsulated the patient during the aversive training. The California psychologist later abandoned the contraption because, as he puts it, his "malpractice insurance carriers were not too impressed . . ."

"Rapid smoking," "forced chain-smoking" or "satiation smoking" (during which you are expected to puff twice as many cigarettes as usual) all intensify and accelerate the effects of the gases, speeding up your heart beat and punching you in the stomach until you almost throw up. (Some patients have actually vomited.) Likewise, the newer machines that blast smoke clouds into your eyes and nostrils operate on a similar aversive principle. As your eyes begin to sting and water, and your lungs rebel with violent coughs, your subconsciousness picks up the smoking-is-a-filthy-habit message as well. In the end, for those who really want to quit, cigarettes are made repugnant.

The experience of the phone booth is recalled by a well-known California businessman who wants to remain anonymous. After paying $500, the man was led into his smoking prison. He was told to take out his Marlboros and start puffing away as fast as he could. The victim eventualy found himself choking. The lighted butt was so hot that it felt as if "his tongue were afire." When the Californian finished the next cigarette, he became extremely dizzy. He hoped that the ordeal was over. But it wasn't. He described what happened next: "After ten drags, I was so dizzy that I could barely keep myself sitting upright on the chair. The therapist told me to put the cigarette out and light another. Soon my hands, feet and legs felt numb and damp."

As the man started his third Marlboro, he was asked if his stomach was upset. "Not yet!" he replied. But a moment later, he could taste bile backing up into his throat.

He gave a signal that he had had enough. He was allowed outside. He felt disoriented. His face looked ashen in the mirror. Other patients have actualy fainted.

While such ordeals obviously leave a mark in anyone's memory, there are physical consequences, too. Are these aversive techniques safe? A number of physicians at the University of Colorado Medical Center say that so much carbon monoxide severely impairs the blood's oxygen-carrying ability. In short, such forced smoking could lead to a heart attack if you already suffer from heart disease. "Rapid smoking should only be risked after a pulmonary lung function test and an EKG (heart test)," says one doctor.

A four-year study at the Pennsylvania State University utilized a special chamber for the research. The doctor in charge said, "Higher nicotine cigarettes yielded significantly greater increases in heart rate and cardiac output. Age differences were noted only in heart rate, with younger subjects having higher reponses to rapid smoking. Rapid smoking produced greater increases in heart rate, systolic and diastolic blood pressure, carboxyphemoglobin, end-tidal CO and a decrease in skin temperature than either rapid breathing or casual smoking."

Another experiment had some unforeseen results. A group of forty-eight science students were made to smoke in a small room. A metronome paced their puffs. While coughing and complaining of the usual nicotine-caused symptoms, the students were told that they should come back for more of the same the following week.

To the doctor's surprise, one half of them never showed up for seconds.

For once, the poisonous weed had had its say.

10

New Ideas

This is the age of alternative medicine, of new approaches, new ideas. You hear much about "wellness"; the expression came to us from "Holistic Medicine," which emphasizes the prevention of disease and treats the "whole" person.

Our present-day healers include the acupuncturists.

As everyone knows by now, acupuncture arrived in the Western world from China, where it has been practiced for 5000 to 6000 years. According to its practitioners, all our physical and mental problems—pain, addictions, cravings, illness—are the result of energy imbalances. Acupuncturists speak of energy movements and of "energy pathways"; they claim that they can rebalance your "energy flow." This is done by means of hair-thin, stainless steel (or silver) needles.

Experienced, professional acupuncturists have never broken a needle nor caused a patient an infection. Bleeding is rare. The treatments are relatively painless for most people, and result in a soothing effect on the mind. Smokers may experience various benefits including relief from the nicotine withdrawal symptoms of nervousness, insomnia, depression and food cravings. Increased willpower to resist cigarettes is also noticed by some people. The immediate effect of an acupuncture treatment usually appears as an overall feeling of relaxation and tension release, with the patient falling into a sound sleep once the needles are removed.

Many smokers have managed to quit after the first twenty-minute session but the experts suggest at least six treatments. Rates vary, depending on locale and the experience of the practitioner. (A visit may cost from $25 to $125.)

The American Medical Association (AMA) still does not officially endorse acupuncture. And while the Germans, Austrians and French enthusiastically have practiced this Chinese therapy for many years, American physicians chose to remain cool to the idea.

This began to change in 1972. That year, members of North America's medical community accepted an invitation to go to China. There, the eminent doctors witnessed acupuncture in person. They returned home convinced about the merits of Chinese medicine. A British team, which went to China at the same time, was equally impressed. As a result, acupuncture is now accepted in many quarters. In California, for instance, there are more than 600 licensed acupuncturists, including many doctors. And, some Chinese experts have meanwhile come to study at the UCLA's Pain Research Center. Despite the above developments, you will not find acupuncturists in every state because their licensing to practice depends on state laws.

Does acupuncture really work for smokers? U.S. government health researchers claim that it is too early to come up with cure statistics. But the *American Journal of Acupuncture* reports an 80 percent success rate for a 5000-person sample; even individual acupuncturists, in separate bookkeeping, registered success rates of 84 percent. Remarkably, too, in most (75 percent) of the cases, "nicotine detoxification" (and abstention) took place after one acupuncture session.

Individual ex-smokers swear by the needle. One of them is longtime California journalist and editor Alan Rich. He said, "I was going through four or five packs of unfiltered Camels a day; I could smoke a pack with one hand while typing with the other and never even know it. The doctor stuck needles in my external ears, on both sides of my nose, at the base of both thumbs, and on the sides of both knees—five half-hour sessions on consecutive days. I emptied my pockets of cigarettes at the end of the first session and haven't touched one since—or felt the need to."

For more information about acupuncture, write: *American Journal of Acupuncture*, 1400 Lost Acre Dr., Felton, CA 95018.

Staple-Puncture

Acupuncturists have also discovered that in some cases, tiny steel balls or a one-sixteenth-inch surgical steel device could also do the trick. Apparently, of all the 200 or so acupuncture points in the human body, the best spot for the pin is your ear. The procedure is known as "auriculotherapy." You will find that most acupuncturists are familiar with it; moreover, some specialized habit-breaking centers have sprung up in North America. Among them are the national ACUTAC Centers, where Dr. M. Anthony Smith answered all my questions:

Casewit: Is the process painful?

Smith: No. There is usually no discomfort. However, the ear may be slightly tender for awhile after it is installed.

Casewit: When does it start working?

Smith: Some people experience an immediate *response*, but most get results within three days.

Casewit: How can I get the best results?

Smith: Whenever you get the urge to smoke, you *must* press on the "Acutac" with the pad of your index finger for a few seconds. If you don't, your ear will get used to the staple being there and you won't get a response.

Casewit: What kind of response can I expect?

Smith: Smokers notice that their craving cigarettes has decreased and/or cigarettes do not taste good.

Casewit: How does the "Acutac" stay in place?

Smith: A piece of tape is placed firmly over it.

Casewit: Does the method work for everyone?

Smith: We've found that approximately 85 percent get results.

Bear in mind that not all acupuncturists agree with the staple treatments. They are still somewhat controversial.

The Norman Ford System

Norman Ford, who is equally at home in Florida, Mexico and in Boulder, Colorado, has been a life-long health researcher and health faddist. He has authored many books on wellness; his best-known work is *Minding Your Body* (see Bibliography). He has also written for numerous health magazines.

In his many years of research, Norman Ford has come up with an interesting new concept. He suggests that one of the best ways to quit smoking is to start fasting.

He recommends a five-day fast, "during which the body undergoes such powerful biochemical changes that cigarettes become repugnant to the taste." Ford points to the euphoria of fasting "which changes life completely: smoking becomes unimportant." And one of the reasons it works is because most people can't smoke on a totally empty stomach without getting sick.

The creator of this theory fasts periodically for five days himself. While he drinks only water during this period, Ford suggests that you drink some fresh, unsweetened juice each morning. And what happens to your body during the five days? Ford says that during the fast, your entire organism excretes accumulations of nicotine more rapidly than by any other method. Withdrawal symptoms are minimal. When you fast, you quickly sense that stimulants will only destroy the wonderful feeling of lightness and freedom that comes with not eating. Your taste buds are totally transformed during a fast. Even after you begin to eat again, cigarettes, snuff, alcohol or coffee will no longer taste good.

An eager skier, climber and hiker, Norman Ford also recommends lots of exercise before, during and after the fast. Exercise fights stress, of course.

Some other experts agree with Ford's system although some of them feel that two days of fasting may be sufficient. Everyone is in accord with starting on this smoking cessation method only when you are *not* under stress. Work pressures must be absent. And, alcohol needs to be cut out for the occasion.

Using Guided Imagery

The Boulder-based health researcher also strongly believes that "Guided Imagery" can be enlisted to quit smoking. What is it and how does it work? Norman Ford explains: "It simply means guiding your mind to imagine vivid pictures of desired health goals. This includes getting rid of the nicotine habit."

Guided Imagery requires your being relaxed and in a quiet environment. This is essential so that you can concentrate and muster all the imaginative powers in your command.

Authorities in this field have determined a certain sequence, along with time allotments for each segment.

- Begin by visualizing your smoking addiction (thirty seconds).
- Visualize your body's own healing powers destroying the addiction (eight minutes).
- Visualize yourself in perfect health (seventy-five seconds).
- Picture your life goals as fulfilled and visualize a good self-image (seventy-five seconds).
- Congratulate yourself for taking an active part in your own wellness. Tell yourself you are feeling great. Maintain a strongly positive feeling (seventy-five seconds).

A chronic smoker will have no difficulties conjuring up the right images for his or her "healing powers destroying the addiction." The smoker knows about the blackness of his or her lungs; in his or her mind's eye, he or she can watch them slowly turn pink and firm like a young person's. No more pockmarks; no more dark welts that might turn into tumors. One can easily imagine the redness of an irritated throat, which gradually becomes normal again. And thus with any organ of your choosing. You might even include items you can see: yellowed teeth, for instance, or bleeding gums, stained fingers or cigarette-caused facial wrinkles.

Meditation

Meditation first proved its mettle convincingly with heroin addicts and LSD-users in the San Francisco counter-culture. To the amazement of the staff of several withdrawal clinics, drug addicts could be taught meditation. And meditation worked! The science magazines of the nineteen sixties and seventies are full of laudatory stories about the cured individuals. By 1973 studies at Harvard Medical School and UCLA confirmed that various techniques (including "TM," or Transcendental Meditation) had helped heavy marijuana users and some alcoholics.

It made sense that the same method could also work for nicotine addicts. And while not all of them chucked the habit, many meditators were able to cut down their daily cigarette quota.

To be sure, meditation erases stress. It relaxes the body/mind and thus makes smoking unnecessary.

Physiologists know precisely what a fifteen-minute session will do: It will reduce your heart rate, decrease oxygen consumption, lower blood pressure and stimulate the alpha activity of your brain.

There are a number of specific methods, TM among them. All can be learned quickly and practiced almost anywhere.

What is meditation like? How do you get started? Some people are able to begin sitting cross-legged in Yoga's "lotus position." Less pliable persons simply sit in a straight-backed chair with their feet on the floor.

Achieve some relaxation by breathing deeply. Tighten and release all your muscles. Take more deep, soothing breaths.

Meditators choose a "mantra" or word they can repeat. In some cases it is *om* or *one*, but it can be whatever works for you. Just keep repeating it. Concentrate on it. The word soon shuts out the rest of the world. You begin to relax. You stop all thought. You eventually achieve a deep mental rest. Fifteen to twenty minutes suffice.

Some long-time meditation aficionados swear by this technique. Smokers have nothing to lose by trying it. (For more information, see the Bibliography.)

Biofeedback

What is Biofeedback? You have no doubt heard about this diagnostic tool, this electronic mirror of your physical self. You might describe Biofeedback as a method of helping you to regulate body and mind. This training uses sensitive sophisticated equipment, which attaches to you in painless, noninvasive ways to detect levels of muscle tension, skin temperature, pulse, sweatiness of the palms. (These areas represent the most easily observable stress reaction sites in your body.)

You can learn more about your heart rate, and your brain waves as well, and this knowledge is fed back to you through visual and auditory signals. (You hear bleeps and see flashing lights.) In time, after enough sessions (that last from thirty to sixty minutes each), you manage to control your stress responses. Eventually, you can achieve relaxation without the equipment.

James R. Craig, a psychologist who employs Biofeedback, sees it simply as a "positive, independent and nondestructive method for coping with stress. After training, the subjects are able to more calmly handle difficult situations that arise in their lives."

Biofeedback has had some remarkable applications. It is regularly used against chronic headaches and migraines. But the method has also paid off as an adjunct to sex therapy and in the treatment of alcoholics. James Craig is somewhat cautious in making promises to smokers. He puts it this way: "Relaxation is rarely enough by itself to cause a smoker to quit, but it is a necessary supplement to any stop-smoking method, since it may replace the only stress management tool owned by the former smoker—cigarettes."

Yet some two-pack-a-day people who were interviewed for this book dispute the psychologist's statement; they swear that Biofeedback did the trick. Other smokers say that they lost "the desire for chain-smoking" and can now get along on two or three cigarettes a day.

To be sure, Biofeedback has its adherents. A Vermont woman with a long history of high blood pressure feels that the treatment has totally changed her life. Here is how she explains it:

> To me, the most serendipitous gift of biofeedback relaxation training has been the amount of energy it gave me—physical, sexual, creative energy. It was incredible to me. I was sixty-two years old, yet I felt surges of strength race through my body, such strength as I had not felt since I was in college. The waves of energy came at odd unexpected moments— lying in bed, sitting at a concert, cooking dinner. They made me more productive. I could do more efficiently. I was more centered. I had greater staying power.

In a more direct way, another kind of Biofeedback has been utilized by the New Hampshire Lung Association to attack cigarette smoking among high school students. Lung associations in Georgia and Virginia have also worked along similar lines. One of the Lung Association's officials tells about the modus operandi: "This project emphasizes smoking's immediate effects on the body. Using a carboximeter to measure the amount of carbon monoxide in the breath, a digital heart rate monitor to measure pulse rate, a digital thermometer to measure skin temperature, and a homemade 'tremor tester', students can see firsthand how cigarettes impair manual control, increase pulse rate, lower skin temperature, and increase carbon monoxide in breath."

The Biofeedback equipment is delivered to a school on Friday afternoon by a staff member of the lung association. Approximately two hours are spent training the science teacher to use the equipment and providing information on smoking.

The following week, students spend fifty minutes each day in an appropriate science class discussing the scientific method as the basis for the week's experiments, reviewing the long- and short-term effects of smoking and using the equipment. Data are collected on smokers before and after smoking a cigarette (parental permission is required). Nonsmokers are also tested twice, serving as controls. In the final period of the week students present the data, draw conclusions and relate findings to general health considerations. The teacher provides additional information on physiology and smoking. A lung association staff member returns to pick up the equipment and delivers it to another school at the end of the week.

Results? According to the New Hampshire Lung Association, 47 percent of the youngsters involved quit at once; of these 32 percent were still off cigarettes six months later.

Shifting Priorities: Exercise as a Cessation Method

As I write these lines, I've just returned from a brisk six-mile mountain walk. We walked in gently undulating terrain—on the same paths we use for cross-country skiing in winter. This is late spring and the pussy willows show their white heads. The first tiny buds have sprouted from the aspen trees. Along the trail, after months of snow, the firs and spruce look greener than ever. We stride on, taking it all in, over hill and dale. Deep breaths of mountain air. Clear sky. Wellness.

A plea for hiking? You bet! This is also a plea for calisthenics, tennis, racquetball, swimming, skiing, cycling, jogging, running or whatever turns you on. If you smoke, exercise helps you shift priorities. You switch to sports instead. Sports demand good breathing, and as you begin to make greater demands on your lungs, you are bound to smoke less, or quit altogether. What's more, exercise works well with other cessation programs.

Vigorous physical effort is the "in" thing these days. Reasons? It helps release tension. It restores mental and emotional balance. (People who believe in Yoga claim that smoking is an "imbalance" and can be cured with Yoga exercises.)

Some brief pointers from the latest research of the National Heart, Lung and Blood Institute. Dr. Robert Levy, one of its directors, advises that you build up slowly. If you have been inactive for a long while, remember it will take time to get into shape. But no matter where you begin, you will be able to build up your stamina or pace as your body becomes more fit. Just remember that you will feel more fit after a few weeks than when you first started.

How often should you exercise? Many people believe that once on Sunday is enough. According to Dr. Levy and to many other experts, these weekend athletes are wrong. The Institute recommends at least three sessions a week. Dr. Levy says, "Exercising *regularly* is one of the most important aspects of your program. If you don't exercise at least three times a week, you won't experience as many of the benefits of regular, vigorous physical activity as you could, or make as much progress. Try to spread your sessions throughout the week to maximize the benefits."

Personally, after I stopped smoking more than a decade ago, I opted for daily activity. It might just be a quick one-mile walk to the store; it can also be a thirty-minute lap swim, a hardy workout in the gym, or a two-set singles tennis game. Like many people who are dedicated to an active life, I must do something every day. Exercise as an addiction? Perhaps so. But it certainly beats the smoking addiction!

11

A Cornucopia of Products

Apart from aversive techniques, hypnosis, acupuncture, group cessation programs, there are also the self-help methods that rely on various products. Among these are filters that help you taper off; drugs that act as a substitute for nicotine; deterrent pharmaceuticals, nicotine chewing gum, tranquilizers, and pep pills instead of cigarettes. All in all, experts estimate that the smoking cessation business amounts to some $100 million a year.

Let's take a look at the cornucopia of products, one by one.

Filters

You've seen movie stars with long cigarette holders. Some of the latter may have concealed a "filter," which reduces the tars and nicotine levels of the cigarette. Your favorite drug store—or chain pharmacy—sells all kinds of filters that might be helpful. In one brand, each device is to be used for a full week's smoking. In the competing brand, the filter is used for two weeks. The instructions state, "After eight weeks you will be physiologically capable to quit smoking if you desire. Or you can continue to smoke with Filter Four and substantially reduce the harmful effects of smoking." Customer satisfaction is guaranteed; dissatisfied users can obtain a full refund of the purchase price.

Another Stop Smoking Kit consists of forty-four disposable filters, which gradually remove up to 96 percent of cigarette tar and 88 percent of nicotine, according to promotional literature. One filter is used each day.

Some devices are supposed to be thrown away; others are to be reused. Some have limits for their useful life, such as twenty cigarettes, after which you dispose of them.

All these products sold better in the old days before the filter cigarettes were on the scene, before the Kents, Carltons, Benson & Hedges, Parliament Lights with their reduced tars. Even so, the cigarette holder method—with its "Water Pik," "Venturi," "Nu-Life," "Tar-Gard" and "Aqua-Filter"—can't hurt and will keep some of those noxious elements out of your lungs.

To be sure, the idea behind the filters is that the smoker can be gradually weaned off cigarettes over a period of time, and is then, according to the manufacturers, "best able to stop smoking altogether." (The "best" method— and undoubtedly the quickest—is to stop immediately, but filters do reduce your exposure to the dangerous substances in tobacco smoke.)

Undoubtedly, new brands will show up in this field. Considering the cost of cigarettes, the price for filters is right, so long as they really help you.

Deterrents

You can buy nonprescription stop-smoking drugs that contain nicotine substitutes; these may satisfy your craving for the real thing. You may also want to consider the smoking "deterrents," a form of oral aversion medicine. Some generations ago, parents would wash out a naughty child's mouth with soap; now more sophisticated substances are used to combat alcoholism and other addictions.

According to one of America's foremost government researchers, Dr. J.L. Schwartz, the successful use of medication to cure illnesses, addictions and unwanted habits has led to its use as an aid in smoking cessation.

Smoking deterrents, such as astringent mouthwashes, are prepared mainly from silver nitrate, copper sulfate or potassium permanganate. These preparations create their deterrent effect by irritating the inside of your mouth. Other products, aimed at diminishing the sensory drives, are bitters prepared from quinine or quassia, local anesthetics in the form of benzocaine lozenges, taste substitutes made from assorted flavors and substances such as atropine or stramonium that create a dry mouth.

One researcher also tested an anti-smoking lozenge that contained asafetida, a gum resin from roots of a plant that has a garlicky odor and acidy taste. The lozenge is placed under the tongue whenever the patient smokes, creating a nauseating taste and odor. Result: the smoker is turned off by tobacco.

Most of the test people stopped smoking after a week or longer. A government report states that the success rate after four years proved to be a high 67 percent. Unfortunately, for some unknown reason—perhaps the FDA's slowness—drug companies did not jump on the band wagon to get the product on the market.

Drugs

Dr. Schwartz's research indicates that there are presently two kinds of pharmaceutical agents to help people quit smoking: agents developed specifically to help smokers overcome the habit and drugs prescribed to help persons overcome withdrawal problems. Two types of pharmaceuticals are aimed at the smoking habit: substitutes and vegetable base products. Lobeline sulphate is the most common smoking substitute; its purpose is to serve as a replacement for nicotine. Some of the lobeline base products (tablets and lozenges) are sold under the "Bantron" and "Nikoban" label by your pharmacist. These products ape some of the nicotine kicks by stimulating your heart rate and respiratory system. Lobeline may thus satisfy the smoker's hunger for a cigarette and eventually help him or her to go on the nicotine-free wagon. According to Dr. Schwartz' research, another drug, made from laburnum, a poisonous plant, is also claimed to be a nicotine substitute; it is used in Bulgaria, Poland and Germany.

Most scientists point out that the success rate of all these remedies varies from group to group and person to person; after all, the smoker will also have to fight his or her psychological addiction as well. This fight may include the use of a "dummy cigarette" with menthol flavors, sold by some stores.

So much for nicotine substitutes. Now how about specific drugs to fight the withdrawal symptoms? When I still smoked, my doctor prescribed some (then most welcome) amphetamines such as Benzedrine and Dexetrine. Both are known as "pep pills." The doctor's rationalization? If the patient is deprived of the brain-and-circulation-proding cigarettes, he or she must need something else instead, i.e., pep pills. Results? I continued to smoke while also getting high on amphetamines, a double dose of stimulation. Eventually, the good doctor's prescription ran out and the "5-Day Plan" helped me quit for good.

Numerous other possibilities exist, including many dubious ones. Physicians have prescribed drugs of all kinds to combat the withdrawal pains. Some medicines have a relaxing effect, others help the patient sleep or overcome nervousness, while others work to prevent weight gain or fatigue. Drug types include anticholinerics, sedatives, tranquilizers, sympathomimetics and anticonvulsants. Dr. Schwartz considers all of them of doubtful value.

In France, meanwhile, a lozenge named "Nicoprive" is sold in pharmacies. It contains a bitter-tasting quinine deterrent plus vitamins B-1 and B-6. And in Germany, Switzerland and Austria, you can buy "Nicobrevin," another well-named drug. It consists of camphor, vitamin C, B-1, eucalyptus and a small amount of ether. Likewise, injections of vitamins, minerals and lobeline hydrochloride have been tried, especially in Sweden.

A Nicotine Chewing Gum?

In Sweden, a "nicotine chewing gum" has also been invented to combat the urge for the real thing. The gum is marketed not only in Sweden, but also in the United Kingdom, Germany, Switzerland and other countries under the "Nicorette" label. A similar product will soon be available throughout the Soviet Union. The price of the gum is reasonable enough. And it seems to work well for people who want to reduce the number of cigarettes they smoke each day. With some luck, they can stop chewing after about one month, and stay off cigarettes, as well.

While real nicotine zaps your brain within seconds, "Nicorette" takes several minutes to do the job. It requires another twenty to thirty minutes to release all the nicotine content of the gum, which is currently being sold on prescription in Canada. Adverse effects? A little heartburn, acceleration of your circulatory system, increased production of your stress hormones— not much better for you than the genuine article.

In the U.S., the FDA is in the process of checking out the chewing gum. In the end, all these drugs and deterrents still demand something else of the user: The *willpower* to stop smoking for good.

12

Victory!

You have decided to quit. You have *chosen* not to smoke any longer. The actual cessation method doesn't matter. Only the fact that you are now out there, not just partially abstinent, which would probably lead you back to the old habits, but totally abstinent.

You have not touched a cigarette for more than two hours. Just what sort of obstacles can you expect during that first morning, and the next few days?

Expect a few withdrawal symptoms. Psychological ones as well as physiological ones. The extent of these symptoms varies from individual to individual. But by and large, the severity has been exaggerated. You were not a heroin addict; you were a smoker.

Personally, I felt the deep exhilaration of having decided against self-abuse, of having opted for the new healthy life. Even after just a smokeless morning, I felt sure that I could do it.

To succeed, it is necessary to be positive about your resolve. If you muster your self-confidence, you cannot be derailed. A clear understanding of your motivations for quitting also helps. Dr. Brengelmann, the German expert, points this out, too. "The most important thing is to remember what sort of *gains* you'll make through your abstention. Keep those gains in mind during those first days."

A positive attitude also helps you to revamp your daily habits. Do this at once: Avoid the places where you used to smoke. In my case, for instance, I temporarily left my office—where I used to fill ashtray after ashtray—and worked outdoors. Luckily, it was summer; I began to write at a large picnic table in the garden, fragrant with the scents of flowers and freshly cut grass, not far from the cherry tree and the bushes laden with raspberries.

Coping With Psychological Withdrawal

Dr. L. M. Ramirez, an expert in psychological withdrawal symptoms claims that the smoking habit is associated for many with reading and writing. Smokers often smoke while simultaneously reading, writing and thinking. "You smoked during this activity because you wanted to review and think about your work. You felt smoking would help you think out a problem. We suggest you study—or work—in an area where you have fresh air circulating. There should not be any cigarettes or ashtrays in sight. When you get the urge to smoke, stand up and stretch. Walk around."

Naturally, all the old habit patterns need to be broken, and broken consciously. If you smoked while watching football games on TV, you need to ask your spouse, lover or friend to accompany you to a movie instead. Generally, you cannot smoke in movie theatres.

Not to smoke must become a game, a challenge, something you actually enjoy doing. If you make it an amusing game, you'll be able to resist people who foolishly offer you a cigarette. "No thanks," you'll say. "I've just quit."

Every move has to be planned. On a recent railway trip through Italy's Po Valley, en route to Venice, I got to talking with an Italian professor who was off the weed for only four hours. We conversed in the corridor, and after half an hour, he excused himself. He wanted to read his newspaper. He mistakenly chose a smoking compartment on the train.

Curious, I observed him for a while through the glass doors. In ten minutes or so, he reached for his *sigaretta*, and was smoking again. The American Cancer Society researchers could have predicted the outcome in that smoking compartment. The ACS experts offer the following suggestions:

You avoid carrying matches or a lighter.

You spend time in places where smoking is prohibited, such as in a library, theater, museum. Lunch with friends who are also trying to quit smoking, at a restaurant with a "no smoking" section.

You treat yourself well. Indulge in a bath, massage, nap, your favorite music, a play. (You don't need a cigarette to have a good time.)

And that you keep your hands occupied—doodling, knitting. Use a calculator to see how much you're saving by not smoking. Some people play with toothpicks; others use pipe cleaners or even silly putty.

One ACS doctor says, "If you can get through the first day, the next will be easier, and easier, and easier. Until after a while the urge to smoke will leave you and you'll wonder why you didn't quit years ago."

Physical Withdrawl Symptoms

According to Dr. Kenneth Cooper, in a research paper for the ACS, "psychological withdrawal is easy to deal with. Nicotine, the addictive substance in tobacco, is largely eliminated from the bloodstream and body tissues via the kidneys. To promote this flushing effect and decrease the craving for cigarettes, a high liquid intake—especially fruit juices—is desirable."

Dr. Cooper is supported in this theory by almost all the cessation programs; the 5-Day Plan physicians, for instance, make it a point to recommend gallons of orange juice during those first few days. Perrier and tap water, mint tea or apple cider are also excellent. Coffee is to be avoided at all costs, since coffee will stimulate you to reach for a cigarette.

According to the Cooper study, the first three to four days are the most difficult, since the bulk of nicotine is being eliminated; most individuals will also experience the real withdrawal symptoms that are related to the effects on the autonomic nervous system.

Moderate to severe headaches, irritability, muscle aches and cramps, anxiety, visual and sleep disturbances, along with an intense craving for tobacco, have been reported by those who are quitting smoking. Dr. Cooper writes: "Generally the peak in severity of symptoms is reached by the third or fourth day. However, symptoms, when present, are highly individualized, and a significant number of those who stop state that they have few, if any, symptoms. For example, some persons state that they have problems with daytime drowsiness and lethargy while others relate that they suffer from insomnia."

When the Craving Begins

Personally, I found the first day the most difficult; this is understandable because I'd been a tobacco fiend for almost thirty years. (A few other oldtimers speak of "climbing the walls" during the first few hours.) It is fortunate that the craving comes in waves and lasts only seconds. Resist the temptation to light up during those few moments. Substitute another treat— some interesting seasonal fruit like strawberries, for instance, or some grapes. One expert advises: "You miss the calming effect of cigarettes. You may feel short-tempered. Try to be outdoors as much as possible and you will not feel like smoking so much. Eat an apple or chew sugar-free gum when the craving for cigarettes begins."

You will be surprised by the speed with which the craving passes, particularly if you learn to distract yourself. Of course, enough time is essential, which is why some people begin to abstain on a weekend, or when they go on vacation. Sports are among the best tension relievers, especially for persons to whom athletics are important. In my case, I simply increased the length of my mountain hikes and the number of sets on the tennis court. Joggers or runners are also lucky in that respect; they can easily escape the cigarette craving.

At a Cessation Program of the Xerox Corporation, in Webster, New York, the quitter is asked to *walk* instead of driving. After all, walking is excellent exercise. Specifically, the Xerox health specialists suggest:

- Walk to the neighborhood grocery store instead of driving.
- Go to the mail box instead of sending the kids.
- Park several blocks from the office and walk.
- Walk up one flight of stairs and down two, instead of using elevators.
- If practical, cut your lawn with a push lawnmower, do not ride.
- Take a walk break, instead of a coffee break.

The Continental Health Enhancement Center Deep Relaxation System

If you are not in good health and therefore cannot exercise, or are not used to it, you can still fight the withdrawal stresses in another way. You can breathe deeply whenever the nicotine urge gets to you.

Most people breathe too shallowly; which is why Dr. Paul Hansen, on the staff of a well-known western health center, makes it a point to explain deep breathing in detail. Dr. Hansen says that "deep relaxation is accomplished through total utilization of the breath, which enables us to control portions of the autonomic nervous system. We breathe automatically without thinking of it, and yet we also have voluntary control over our breathing process."

These are the Health Center's breathing exercises:

1. Deep breathing: breathe with the entire lung capacity in such a manner that the abdomen distends prior to the expansion of the ribcage, followed by the expansion of the upper lung and a slight elevation of the shoulders. Deep breathe in that sequence so that the air goes to the bottom of the lungs first. A deep breath or several deep breaths is a good initial relaxation tool.

2. Take about thirty complete deep breaths. As you inhale, say to yourself silently "I am," and as you exhale say to yourself "relaxed."

3. Breathe to your primary area of tension. Create an image in your mind of a flexible air tube extending from your nasal passages to your primary muscle groups where you hold tension. As you inhale, imagine you are breathing in pure oxygen to that muscle group, and as you exhale, imagine that the tension is flowing out through your nose like black smoke.

4. Breathe through your primary area of tension. Imagine that the muscle cells in your tense areas have suddenly separated enough so that air can be drawn through them and through the skin into the lungs as you inhale, and that as you exhale the air is expelled right through the muscle and out through the skin.

5. Slow your breathing to four times a minute. Watch a clock while you are breathing and gradually slow the breathing to the point where you

make one inhalation and exhalation every fifteen seconds. This will induce a deep state of relaxation.

Personally, I found that the deep breathing technique really helps chase away the craving and relaxes you. A trip to the mountains, the ocean or the unpolluted midwestern regions would be helpful, too.

Staying off the Weed

Experts claim that the physical symptoms decrease after eight to ten days; for some people, even sooner. Are you cured then? Actually, not yet. There still await far too many relapse possibilities. Nonsmoking takes practice.

Life is hectic and harsh in the 1980s, and despite one's commitment, one may suddenly reach for the old crutch again. According to one serious study of "backsliding," undertaken on behalf of *Psychology Today*, backsliding can occur to "cope with a person's negative emotional state: frustration, anger, guilt, fear, loneliness, depression. The person may have felt hassled, apprehensive or simply bored. In each case, the old habit was resumed for relief."

The researchers also found that some quitters cannot resist the "powerful social pressures." They light up when others do, because they fear that they may be ostracized for abstaining. Such an obstacle can be overcome, however, by sticking obstinately to your nonsmoking stance. Tell the person: "I'm sorry. I've made a resolution. And I can't smoke."

The dangers exist, of course. Unlike some European countries, the U.S. and Canada tolerate cigarette machines. And magnificent billboads proclaim the companionable aspects of tobacco. Dr. J. Nguyen, a well-known acupuncturist, has amassed much experience with smokers and their habit. Like his colleagues elsewhere, Dr. Nguyen warns,

> Our long-term advice to smokers is simple. We emphasize that if they wish to remain cured they must not allow themselves to fall into the trap of lighting a cigarette—not even after a long time after treatment—at special occasions such as a celebration or a party, or in a dramatic situation. Our experience has shown that a single cigarette will often prompt the smoker to restart his habit, although he may have abstained for many years. After interviewing hundreds of previous smokers on their smoking history, we have coined this aphorism: An ex-smoker is a potential smoker. In short, hang in there and you'll be O.K.

The Ex-Smoker's Diet

Quitting means improved tastebuds. You notice this immediately: Eat a plate of asparagus or a chunk of Maine lobster. The most subtle forgotten flavors come back to you, in a rush. Everything suddenly tastes so much better.

This is a joy with a mixed blessing. For some people, it means that they shift from tobacco to food. They gorge themselves. One woman of my acquaintance quit smoking successfully. But she gained weight. This upset her so much that she once more went back to her Virginia Slims and was hooked anew.

All the experts I consulted about weight gain held the same opinion. It didn't matter. Not at this stage, anyway. Dr. Neil Solomon, one of the leading authorities in the field, puts it this way: "Smoking is far worse for your health than a little extra weight," he says. And Bobbie Jacobsen, a British cessation and diet expert, asks quitters, especially women, to answer four questions:

- How will my life change if I gain a few pounds?
- Why am I preoccupied with being thin?
- Whom am I trying to please by striving to stay thin?
- Is it more important to please others than to restore my health?

Moreover, recent research confirms that only about one-third of the quitters add pounds; the others—especially the consistent exercisers—lose weight, or remain at the same level. Dr. Solomon found that most ex-smokers will "plateau" for two months and lose any added pounds after five months.

It is also true that you cannot fight on two fronts at the same time. Go on the nicotine wagon first, and stay on it for a few months. If you've put a few pounds on by then, you can take the next steps, i.e., dieting.

To be sure, you can't go wrong eating fresh fruit and fresh vegetables, with grains, nuts, sunflower-seeds; by contrast, avoid peppery foods, Mexican dishes, spicy meats and liquor, which all stimulate you to smoke again.

Many doctors recommend plenty of vitamin C in pill form, too; and extra doses of other vitamins, particularly the B-complex. This is the vitamin to help your nicotine-deprived nerves. You can get B-complex in tablet form or by eating wheat germ.

Cigarettes used to provide oral gratification; for in-between snacks, you now need a replacement. Apart from juices, try sugarless gum, dietetic candy, carrot sticks, beef jerky and other nonfattening items.

Taking lots of baths helps you stay relaxed. One recent comic strip character, in his struggle to quit cigarettes, did just that. He bathed all the time. He bathed so much that he felt, as he said, "like Jacques Cousteau."

13

The Advantages of Being a Nonsmoker

Not long ago, at the San Juan (Puerto Rico) Airport, I saw a man put one dollar and fifty cents' worth of quarters into the cigarette machines. Expensive! Even if you only pay $1 per pack and smoke two packs a day, you're shelling out $60 a month for cigarettes. A wizard at the University of Southern California once figured out that the average consumer also spends about $37.00 a year for matches, lighters, fluid, ashtrays and other smoking-related materials. The Report: "Over the next 20 years, the price of cigarettes and related items will continue to rise, just as they have over the last 20 years. Assuming an average inflation rate of 7.5 percent (wouldn't that be nice), the average cost of a pack of cigarettes over the 20 year period will be $1.98 and the amount spent on related items will average $92.00 a year.

"That means that over the next 20 years, the typical smoker will spend about $723 a year on cigarettes alone and another $92.00 on related items. The total direct cost of smoking over the next 20 years will be about $16,300."

All the above applies only to North America; most Europeans have to pay even more. In the same vein, revenue-eager British, Swedish, German, French and other governments keep hiking cigarette taxes. In the U.S., some states now include 40ᶜ for assorted taxes per pack.

Now that you've stopped, the savings are considerable; $16,300 in twenty years buys you a trip around the world or a snazzy automobile, to give just two examples.

There are other financial considerations. Many leading insurance companies sell you automobile insurance at a reduced cost if you don't smoke. Likewise, nonsmokers, or reformed smokers, are eligible for life insurance premium discounts of up to 22 percent if they have not smoked cigarettes for at least twelve months. In 1964, State Mutual Life Assurance Company of Worcester, Massachusetts, issued the first such policy for nonsmokers. This was quickly followed by some 100 other companies.

Moreover, a number of U.S. companies pay a bonus to workers who quit the habit. A printer in St. Louis, Missouri, for example, who lost many employees to assorted cancers, now offers $600 to anyone who quits. The check is handed out two months after the person quits. Provided they don't start up again, of course.

Non-Smoking Offices

It is also true that the nonsmoker has an easier time in getting a job with many companies. Certain firms actually refuse to hire tobacco addicts; one typical example is Rodale Press, a publisher in the health field. None of its 800 employees are allowed to smoke at work. There are other excellent examples to illustrate many employers' prejudice against smokers. One of Seattle's largest technology companies, for instance, hands out application forms where the question, "Do you smoke?" is underlined in red. The same pro-health attitudes apply to other fields, including retail, service and financial firms. Interestingly, it is *not* illegal to discriminate against smokers. According to the Equal Employment Opportunity Commission, discrimination only comes up in cases of religion, sex, age or national origin. In short, no one needs to hire a smoker any longer. Personally, I refuse to work with typists who favor cigarettes.

To be sure, employers have their own good reasons for this pro-health stance. In one typical study, cigarette users become ill four times more often than abstainers. The study also maintained that the cigarette consumers are also first in line to catch colds and they are absent from work for other medical reasons more than non-smokers. It has also been found that productivity and employee morale improve in a smoke-free atmosphere.

Dr. William Weis, a personnel expert, once figured out that cigarette use costs the employer a great deal. Dr. Weis said, "Estimates of on-the-job time lost to the smoking ritual—lighting, puffing, staring, pretending to be in deep thought, informal breaks—vary among sources, ranging from a low of eight minutes per day to a high of 15 to 30 minutes per hour. A conservative compromise of 30 minutes per day for cigarette smokers and 55 minutes per day for pipe smokers, is the basis for this estimate."

Fires

You're familiar with the daily headlines in your newspaper: "Senior Citizen Burned to Death in Bed!" "Retired Man Fell Asleep With Cigarette—$200,000 Damage!" "Hotel Fire that Kills Forty Started by Smoker!" Or this Philadelphia newspaper story:

SIX CHILDREN DIE IN WEST PHILADELPHIA BLAZE
Six children were killed and three other people, including a sixteen-month-old girl, were injured this morning when a one-alarm fire gutted a two-story home in West Philadelphia.
A cigarette, carelessly left smoldering on a living room couch, caused the blaze...

As a nonsmoker, you no longer risk the above scourges. The facts speak for themselves: The National Fire Protection Association (NFPA) reports that more fatal fires are caused by cigarettes than by any other source of combustion. These fires result in an estimated 2,500 deaths each year in the United States. In addition to the fatalities, an NFPA analysis found that at least 25,000 people were injured during a typical year in residential fires ignited by cigarettes and that approximately $400 million in property was lost in these fires.

One cause for these often catastrophic occurrences? The new cushions, pillows and building materials happen to be more flammable than those of two decades ago. And at least so far, the cigarette companies themselves have not managed to invent a self-extinguishing butt. Instead, a lighted cigarette keeps burning for at least twenty minutes after it has been placed in an ashtray.

And, as with some jobs, the nonsmoker has some advantages when apartment hunting. He or she can often get a choice apartment, which would never be rented to a smoker. Indeed, many landlords are becoming more and more firm in refusing to sign leases with cigarette fiends. And for good reasons: apartment owners fear the fire dangers. Not to mention holes burned in carpets, blackened furniture surfaces or the pervasive smell of stale tobacco.

You may also bear in mind that the atmosphere in your apartment or house becomes more peaceful. It doesn't take a clinical psychologist to conclude that two nonsmoking people get along better than a user and a nonuser. Your spouse or lover will be grateful that you quit. And if one of them is still a smoker, the example of the quitter will help the other still-addicted person. "Kiss me! I don't Smoke!" reads one Cancer Society button.

At Last: Health Regained!

Within twelve hours after you have your last cigarette, your body will begin to heal itself. The levels of carbon monoxide and nicotine in your system will decline rapidly, and your heart and lungs will begin to repair the damage caused by cigarette smoke.

Within a few days, you will begin to notice some remarkable changes in your body. Your sense of smell will return. Your smoker's hack will disappear. Your digestive system will return to normal.

Most important of all, you feel really alive—clear-headed, full of energy and strength. You're breathing easier. You can climb a hill or a flight of stairs without becoming winded or dizzy.

Within a few weeks, your lungs repair themselves; a few months later, their color improves. And a decade afterward, the tissues are like those of a person who never smoked. Your lung cells have regenerated! Dr. George Melcher, who runs the well-respected Continental Health Enhancement Center near Boulder, Colorado, underlines your increased longevity. You won't have to worry so much about lung cancer or other cigarette-related carcinomas. Likewise, your risk of a heart attack has been reduced dramatically. And on a day-to-day basis, there will be sleep improvement, disappearance of headaches and increased stamina.

Naturally, these health incentives will be of little interest to the die-hard nicotine addict. It is obvious that an eighty-year-old who has indulged for a lifetime and is still around, cannot be influenced to quit. He or she somehow has the genes to cope with carbon monoxide and other poisons.

There are also longtime addicts who fool themselves by puffing Kents, Carltons, L&M Lights, Merits and other low-nicotine filter brands. Or they stick to menthol cigarettes like Salems and Kools. None of these brands are "safe," either. And while it's true that the tar content has been lowered through the years, the habit remains as dangerous as two decades ago.

How so? A book-size investigation by the Federal Trade Commission (FTC) came up with some melancholy conclusions. The report states that, "Some of the benefits which might accrue from a reduction in 'tar' and nicotine are to some unknown extent offset by one factor: Many, low 'tar' cigarettes contain flavoring agents and additives to replace the flavor lost by reducing the 'tar' levels. The health effects of these additives and flavoring agents are not yet known and some may themselves be carcinogenic."

What's more, the new-fangled filter cigarettes make some people get started into the habit, and keep others from giving it up. The FTC's explanation: "There is some evidence that the availability of low 'tar' and nicotine cigarettes makes it easier for some people to rationalize not quitting. Based on data indicating that teen-age boys and especially teen-age girls tend to smoke low 'tar' brands in greater proportion than the population at large, one researcher hypothesizes that teen-agers and young adults, particularly girls, find it easier to experiment with and later become habituated to low 'tar' cigarettes."

Lastly, one government medical researcher discovered what may be the weightiest argument against the low-tar brands: "Some smokers who switch from a higher tar to a lower tar-yielding cigarette tend to compensate for this switch. That is, in order to maintain a certain level of nicotine in their blood, these smokers alter their smoking practices either by increasing the number smoked per day or by inhaling deeper or more often."

In fact, what do the health authorities have to say to those who can't seem to quit? Listen to Bobbie Jacobsen, a well-known British expert:

1. Try to inhale as little as possible, although this is easier said than done.

2. Try to take fewer puffs of each cigarette, and make each one short so that you have as little time as possible to inhale.

3. Never smoke the last third of the cigarette—it is the most dangerous part where the tar and toxic materials in the smoke become concentrated. If you are likely to forget, then mark each cigarette beforehand when you open a new pack.

4. Never relight a half-smoked cigarette—however much it offends your sense of waste. When a cigarette goes out, some of the harmful tar condenses and concentrates at the burnt end, and you inhale this when you relight it.

5. Never leave a cigarette in your mouth between puffs. This will minimize the amount you inhale.

The Office on Smoking and Health of the U.S. Public Health Service agrees with the British findings. "Reduce your inhaling and don't inhale as deeply," warns one of the physicians, adding that "you're best off to smoke a cigarette only halfway."

Nonsmokers' Rights

As these words are written, North America's nonsmokers are asserting their rights. They demand that the public heed nonsmoking ordinances and signs. With the help of a Washington-based group named ASH (Action On Smoking and Health), they have persuaded the airlines to assign more seats to abstainers. You can dine at restaurants that ban people with cigarettes. There are now even some motels where smoking is *verboten*. Only nonsmokers are allowed to register.

Because of the ever-increasing health consciousness, individuals nowadays make a stand. It may have begun with Joseph Califano, when he was still HEW Secretary. One day, he received a visit from two Senators from tobacco-growing states. The two men promptly lit up in front of Califano. But the Secretary stood his ground. "I'm sorry," he told them. "There is no smoking in this conference room." The two legislators complied.

Apart from ASH, a large number of other anti-smoking groups have sprung up. GASP (Group to Alleviate Smoking Pollution) is perhaps the most widespread, with chapters in many major cities.

What is GASP's function?

In one city, its members marched on large supermarkets, demanding that the management hang up "Please Do Not Smoke" signs. When one chain refused, the GASP members arranged for a boycott.

In another community, the group hired a doctor to speak to large audiences about the dangers of "sidestream smoke," i.e., the smoke you inhale when someone else lights up near you. Physicians argue that "passive smokers" are in as great a health danger as "active smokers."

In most metropolises, the group monitors each major restaurant, making sure that it offers a nonsmoking section.

Just what can you do when someone else polutes your air? According to GASP, you need to show your disdain.

"Let family, friends, coworkers and strangers know you mind if they smoke. Speak up! If you are shy then at least wear a button. Always ask for a no-smoking section in restaurants and hotels (even if the establishment does not have one). Use suggestion boxes or complaint cards available at most businesses. Put stickers and signs in your car, home and office. Write letters to legislators and other authorities and express your desire for smoke-free areas in public places. Also write letters to your local newspapers."

To be sure, it has become fashionable to fight for your rights. Some people have done so with more enthusiasm than others. Examples? In one eastern city, an employee suggested a nonsmoking section in her large office. When her request was not granted, she came to work in a gas mask. Another purist spoke to the chief librarian at a major metropolitan library about abolishing the "Smoker's Room." No way. On his next library visit, the nonsmoker appeared in the room with smelly Yak incense. When he lit it, the cigarette puffers ran.

Zapping smokers with water pistols has become common on university campuses and in one case, a student even used Windex on his surprised victim. But the most aggressive case concerns a woman in Salt Lake City. She made the news when she appeared in a nonsmoking area with a pair of scissors. She'd ask the offenders to put out their cigarettes. When they didn't, the woman brandished her scissors and snipped the cigarettes in two.

Unusual? Perhaps so. "The pendulum has swung against smokers," says one insider. "At one time the smokers were considered innocents. Now they're considered offenders. And *we* are the not-so-silent majority!"

Addresses of Anti-Smoking Groups

Action for Smoking and Health
2013 H. St. N.W.
Washington, D.C. 20006

Action on Smoking and Health
Education Division
P.O. Box 4339
Takoma Park, MD 20912

California GASP
Main Office
P.O. Box 1061
Berkeley, CA 94701

GASP of Miami
3614 Coral Way
Miami, FL 33145

Group Against Smoking Pollution
P.O. Box 682
College Park, MD 20740

Massachusetts GASP
P.O. Box 842
Brookline, MA 02146

Environmental Improvement Associates
109 Chestnut St.
Salem, NJ 08079

FANS (Fresh Air for Nonsmokers)
Box 24052
Seattle, WA 98124

GASP (Georgians Against Smokers Pollution)
Georgia Lung Association
1383 Spring St. N.W.
Atlanta, GA 30309

New Jersey GASP
105 Mountain Ave.
Summit, NJ 07901

Sacramento GASP
909 12th St.
Lung Assn. of Sacramento
Sacramento, CA 95814

Wichita GASP
P.O. Box 17062
Wichita, KS 67217

14

European Approaches

While the Europeans invented the "Gauloise," the "Rothändle" and the playfully-named "Players" cigarette, some of their pharmaceutical labs also provided a counterweight in the form of drugs discussed in Chapter 11. Interestingly, just as in the U.S., there are now fewer smokers in West Germany, Sweden, Norway and the United Kingdom than twenty years ago. The number of male indulgers has especially decreased in the above countries; in France and Belgium, meanwhile, both men and women abstain in ever greater numbers.

Why should this be so? Keep in mind that the quest for better health and a longer life has invaded the Continent and the U.K. Moreover, some of the governments have waged a long and sincere fight against the cigarette interests. Indeed, what's new in that battle? And how is it fought by the various European nations? Here's a brief accounting:

Sweden: A "Cigarette-Free Society by the Year 2000"

The Swedes have always been in the forefront of the war against tobacco. It began in 1963 when the Swedish government funded its first big smoking control program. A year later, this health-minded Scandinavian country created the "National Smoking and Health Association," or NTS, which launched a campaign "to create a cigarette-free society by the year 2000."

Some of their achievements are remarkable. For instance: tobacco consumption has been whittled down by legislation and persuasion that affects all elements of Swedish life. Limits on tobacco product advertising have been mandated. Ads may be no larger than a 15 centimeter square, must carry the health warnings and content identifications and are limited to daily newspapers and certain weeklies. No television or radio ads are allowed. And the ban on advertising may become even more pervasive. The Swedish

National Board of Health and Welfare has called for a total ban on all tobacco product advertising.

What's more, the ads cannot show the merry scenes that seduce America's youth: the forest-green Salem cigarette landscapes, for instance, or the manly Marlboro cowboys riding into the sunset. Women are not used to sell the product, as in U.S. cigarette ads. Packages only, against a neutral background. This is not exactly the ad person's dream and certainly affects sales.

Another Swedish approach involves labeling all tobacco products with health messages regarding the dangers of smoking. Sixteen such warnings are currently placed on brands marketed in Sweden, and several special warning notices are used for other types of tobacco products. Tar, nicotine, and carbon monoxide contents must be identified!

Among the sixteen warnings on cigarette packages, you can read reminders to mothers that say they should be worried about "nicotine in the bloodstream affecting the fetus"; and, for children of parents who smoke, the messages warn that a smoker's child may be "prone to bronchitis." You'll also discover tidbits such as:

- Lung cancer reaps more victims than road accidents. Most lung cancer deaths can be attributed to smoking.
- Emphysema is a disease of the lung tissue, which can cause breathing difficulties. Mainly affects smokers.
- More and more people are suffering from heart infarction and other vascular diseases. This applies especially to smokers.
- Smokers get ulcers more often than nonsmokers. Ulcers heal faster if you stop smoking.

And many others. The messages may sound familiar and even banal. But they must infuriate the Swedish tobacco merchants.

In Stockholm, the powers-that-be aim frankly at making their children "the first generation of nonsmokers." To do it, a pack of your favorite brand now costs more than $2. The sale of cigarettes from vending machines has been outlawed in Sweden. And sales in food stores is being phased out. Students of all ages are being taught the dangers of these "coffin nails." Elementary and high schools are being bombarded by health professionals with material about the genuine dangers awaiting those who puff away. In Stockholm, the latest fashion is T-shirts with the "Nonsmoking Generation" message, along with billboards partially financed by VISIR: *We som into roker*—We who don't smoke. Midwives and physicians preach the gospel in maternity wards, and even the child-care workers talk about the dangers of smoking to the littlest ones in the children's day schools and recreation centers.

The fervor has already paid off. More and more Swedes have become "non-s's." They are *We som into Roker*.

Norway and Its "Tobacco Act"

And in neighboring Norway? Not to be outdone by the Swedes, the environmentally-conscious Norwegians—those legendary skiers and hikers—pursued their anti-tobacco drives as far back as the early 1960s.

In 1964, "A report of the Norwegian National Council on Smoking and Health at once outlined goals of a national anti-smoking campaign. Educational efforts have been directed chiefly at health professionals and educators, adolescents and schoolchildren, and patients with smoking-related diseases. A network of specially trained field workers has been organized to communicate health information to the public. These workers are equipped with a slide series, 'A Physician Talks About Smoking', and a short textbook, 'Smoking and Health'. Pamphlets are distributed on subjects such as 'The Patient', 'Passive Smoking', and 'Smoking Among Women'. A teacher's guide has been prepared containing educational material."

By 1975, the Norwegians had banned almost all ads for tobacco products. According to federal law, "The Tobacco Act prohibits the advertising of all types of tobacco products, including cigarette paper.

"The prohibition also affects the use of tobacco products in connection with the advertising of other goods. For instance, advertisements for cars or clothes are not to show anyone smoking."

The ban on advertising applies to all media, such as the press, films, neon light advertisements and billboards.

Not long after, the Norwegian "National Council on Smoking and Health" began to wage its own propaganda campaign. The Council announced the availability of a large slide collection covering the various aspects of the smoking and health problem. "Each slide is accompanied by a sheet with comments to make it easy for the field worker to compose slide-series specifically aimed at the target group whom he or she is going to brief. The Council has also bought 200 sets of the slide-series. The slides have been distributed to schools for medical students, nurses, public health nurses, teachers—and to doctors with a special interest in smoking and health programs."

As a result, one of every five males quit. (Unfortunately, in 1981, Norwegian women still continued to smoke at the same rate as before.) The future may change these statistics, though. One reason: a hefty new campaign in schools and no sales of cigarettes to anyone under the age of sixteen.

The U.K.: Another Valiant Battle

If Great Britain had much to do with the introduction of laws as we now know them in North America, Britain was also among the first nations we know of to declare war on tobacco. Indeed, the "English Anti-Tobacco Society" was formed as far back as 1876.

England was among the first countries to kick cigarette ads off the television screen; the ban came in 1965. Throughout the years, the British version of ASH—plus the "Society of Nonsmokers"—became powerful instruments; they declared a "National Don't Smoke Day" and they helped enact a code to restrict print advertising. In fact, it was one of these anti-tobacco organizations that talked Great Britain's version of the (U.S.) Trade Commission into regulating cigarette ads. The code required that advertisements: "Should not seek to encourage people, particularly the young, to start smoking or, if they are already smokers, to increase their level of smoking or smoke to excess; and should not exploit those who are especially vulnerable."

In particular, the code specified that advertisements were no longer allowed to suggest that smoking was "a sign or proof of manliness, or that smokers were more virile or tough than nonsmokers."

The ad code also asked newspapers and magazines to refrain from "Including ad copy of illustrations which are sexually titillating or which imply a link between smoking and sexual success . . . or claim directly or indirectly that to smoke, or to smoke a particular brand, is a sign or proof of courage, or daring."

For more than twenty years, cigarette packs have carried health warnings, and—bad news for cigarette sales people!—prices have risen astronomically. At present, a pack costs two dollars in London. Much of the $2 is for taxes. "The British government is taxing us into quitting," says one disgruntled Londoner.

Unfortunately, as in many other countries, including the U.S., the British government cannot pursue an anti-tobacco policy with too much vigor. Every year, England derives a $2 billion revenue from cigarettes and alcohol. One of the nation's former Health Ministers explained it lucidly enough: "The government finds itself in an embarrassing situation," he said. "On the one hand, it is gathering enormous revenues from the sale of tobacco products. On the other hand, the government is trying to keep the country healthy . . ."

Joseph Califano, former U.S. government official, ran into a similar situation at home. The country's twin interests—staying healthy and catering to tobacco farmers—eventually cost Califano his job.

West Germany: The Turning Tide

The West German government faces a similar dilemma: The Federal and state revenue from cigarettes amounts to almost $5 billion a year; by the same token smoking has become the nation's Number One Health Hazard. If you've ever traveled in West Germany, you must have noticed that everyone seems to smoke—well, *almost* everyone. You spot the young women enjoying their Kents in front of a university; you spy the youthful soldiers amid smoke clouds (80 percent of them indulge). On Germany's airlines, smokers occupy the seats on one side of the plane while the abstainers sit in the other, albeit not too happily because of the fumes drifting across the aisles.

Every hour, two Germans die of lung cancer, and the medical authorities in Bonn warn that *Raucher* (smokers) shorten their lives by 8.3 years. In fact, the Health Ministry bravely tries to tip the scales: large billboards quote the Minister of Health himself: *"Rauchen gefaehrdet Ihre Gesundheit!"* (Smoking endangers your health!).

TV ads have been banned since 1973, and lots of anti-cigarette material is available from the Federal Center For Health Education. Luckily, too, the German version of the Blue Cross—the (Federal) *Krankenkasse*—supplies helpful materials to prospective quitters.

The tide seems to be turning in Germany, too. Some taxi drivers post *Nicht-Raucher* signs and refuse to let a smoker board. And not long ago, a plucky German soldier sued the German army and won the right to a smoke-free barracks environment.

France: Down with "Tabagism!"

French movie stars used to be depicted with their inevitable stubs stuck to their lips. Movie directors couldn't work without a Gitane or a Gauloise in their mouths. Pianists, in films or bistros, couldn't play a note without rolled tobacco. The French call it *Tabagism*. You still see a lot of it on the boulevards, in the parks and at home. Lots of supposed "gourmets" light up after a meal in a Paris restaurant, which is not likely to have a nonsmoking section. Indeed, the French still smoke much more than the Americans.

Fortunately, the French government has not stood still. The planning began in 1974, the attack, a year later. The legislation adopted by the French Parliament made labeling of each cigarette pack mandatory. It also mandated a prominent indication of nicotine and tar contents and the inclusion of the warning "abuse is dangerous." It also totally prohibited smoking in schools attended by students younger than sixteen, in hospitals, clinics, and grocery stores, in children's transportation vehicles, public elevators, and cable railway cars; and restricted smoking in buses, trains, planes and ships. The first campaign of public information on risks was geared to youth and pregnant women. The subsequent campaigns were designed to protect rights and health of passive smokers and to protect the twelve-to eighteen-year-olds from the risks of smoking.

Legislation passed in 1976 prohibits advertising of tobacco and tobacco products by radio, television, recordings or other public announcements; in places of entertainment and other public places; by means of posters, billboards, leaflets, or illuminated or other signs; and free samples may not be distributed for publicity. Tobacco manufacturers and dealers may not sponsor sports events or display the name, brand or advertising symbol of tobacco during a sports event.

In recent years, the Ministry of Health in Paris has released millions of educational brochures and created a yearly nonsmoking day. Ads in magazines can only show packages and no models.

Government posters show a smiling man who drops his white tobacco sticks. "I stop smoking. I live better!" reads the poster. What's more, the French have attacked the habit with auricular acupuncture and assorted pills. And next door, in Belgium, vending machines are now forbidden. Down with *Tabagism!*

Waging the Fight on All Fronts

Obviously, the battle against cigarettes must be waged on all levels. The vigorous Tobacco Lobby in Congress must be fought on the Federal front, harsher warnings must be placed on the sides of cigarette cartons and packages. Non-smokers must also stand up for their rights.

In August of 1982, the *Boston Globe* reported an interesting story about a restaurant owner in Marlborough, Massachusetts, who had taken an unusual action against smokers. It seems that his brother had died of cancer the year before. This sparked the owner into putting up signs thanking people for not smoking. When this failed to "clear the air," the owner put up another sign. This one informed smokers that they could go on polluting but a charge of 25 cents would be added to their bill for every cigarette or cigar they lit up. In eight months, this restaurant owner collected one hundred dollars, all of which was donated to the American Cancer Society.

While this may be the sort of action that only a business owner can take, we can all encourage our friends who are smokers to quit. Or, we can politely ask people not to smoke when we are present. Quite a few non-smokers would agree with one militant non-smoking television actor who says that other people's right to smoke ends where his nose begins.

As more and more companies refuse to hire smokers, as some insurance companies offer reduced costs to abstainers and as municipalities legislate against smoking in public, there are fewer and fewer reasons for anyone to maintain a tobacco habit. And we can all become involved in the fight against cigarettes by helping and encouraging our friends to stop. Remember, while they may complain that we are pestering them or discriminating against them, we will be doing ourselves and them a huge favor in the long run.

Appendix 1

Tar, Nicotine and Carbon Monoxide Content of Two Hundred (200)
Varieties of Domestic Cigarettes
(shown in increasing order of tar values)

BRAND	TYPE	TAR (mg/cig)	Nicotine (mg/cig)	Carbon Monoxide (mg/cig)
Vantage Ultra Lights 100's	100mm, filter	5	0.5	8
Pall Mall Extra Light	king, filter	6	0.5	6
Kool Super Lights	king, filter, menthol	6	0.5	7
Carlton 120's	120mm, filter	6	0.6	6
Vantage Ultra Lights	king, filter	6	0.5	9
Camel Lights	king, filter, hp	6	0.6	7
Merit	king, filter, menthol	7	0.5	10
Tareyton Long Lights 100's	100mm, filter	7	0.6	7
Merit	king, filter	7	0.5	10
Lark Lights 100's	100mm, filter	7	0.6	7
Golden Lights 100's	100mm, filter, menthol	7	0.7	7
Lark Lights	king, filter	7	0.6	7
L & M Lights 100's	100mm, filter, menthol	7	0.8	6
Virginia Slims Lights 100's	100mm, filter, hp	7	0.6	8
Arctic Lights 100's	100mm, filter, menthol	7	0.6	9
L & M Lights 100's	100mm, filter, menthol	7	0.8	6
Virginia Slims Lights 100's	100mm, filter, hp	7	0.6	8
American Lights 120's	120mm, filter	8	0.7	9
Arctic Lights	king, filter, menthol	8	0.6	9
Lucky Ten	king, filter	8	0.6	9
Golden Lights	king, filter, menthol	8	0.7	8
Camel Lights	king, filter	8	0.7	10
American Lights 120's	120mm, filter	8	0.7	9
L & M Lights	king, filter	8	0.7	7
Salem Lights	king, filter, menthol	8	0.6	10
True 100's	100mm, filter, menthol	8	0.6	9
Viceroy Rich Lights	king, filter	8	0.7	10
Belair	king, filter	8	0.7	9
Newport Lights	king, filter, menthol, hp	8	0.7	10
Newport Lights	king, filter, menthol	8	0.8	10
Vantage 100's	100mm, filter	8	0.7	12
Decade 100's	100mm, filter	8	0.8	7
Raleigh Lights	king, filter	8	0.7	11
Golden Lights 100's	100mm, filter	8	0.8	9
Belair 100's	100mm, filter, menthol	8	0.6	10
Parliament Lights	king, filter	9	0.6	10
Parliament Lights	king, filter, hp	9	0.6	10
Vantage	king, filter	9	0.7	13
Merit 100's	100mm, filter, menthol	9	0.7	11

Tar, Nicotine and Carbon Monoxide Content of Two Hundred (200) Varieties of Domestic Cigarettes
(shown in increasing order of tar values)

BRAND	TYPE	TAR (mg/cig)	Nicotine (mg/cig)	Carbon Monoxide (mg/cig)
Viceroy Rich Lights 100's	100mm, filter, menthol	9	0.8	12
Pall Mall Light 100's	100mm, filter	9	0.8	9
Salem Lights 100's	100mm, filter, menthol	9	0.8	11
Raleigh Lights 100's	100mm, filter	9	0.8	13
Kool Super Lights 100's	100mm, filter, menthol	9	0.7	12
Old Gold Lights	king, filter	10	0.9	10
Merit 100's	100mm, filter	10	0.7	12
Benson & Hedges Lights 100's	100mm, filter, menthol, hp	10	0.7	11
Vantage	king, filter, menthol	10	0.7	14
Benson & Hedges Lights 100's	100mm, filter, menthol, hp	10	0.7	11
Marlboro Lights 100's	100mm, filter	10	0.7	12
Marlboro Lights	king, filter, hp	10	0.7	12
Benson & Hedges Lights 100's	100mm, filter	10	0.7	13
Marlboro Lights	king, filter	11	0.7	12
Winston Lights	king, filter	11	0.9	11
Kool Milds	king, filter, menthol	11	0.9	12
Silva Thins 100's	100mm, filter, menthol	11	0.1	9
Silva Thins 100's	100mm, filter	11	0.1	9
Camel Lights 100's	100mm, filter	12	0.9	15
Multifilter	king, filter, menthol	12	0.8	11
Winston Lights 100's	100mm, filter	12	0.9	14
Parliament Lights 100's	100mm, filter	12	0.9	11
Kool Milds 100's	100mm, filter, menthol	12	0.1	13
Multifilter	king, filter	12	0.8	11
Hi-Lite 100's	100mm, filter, hp	12	0.9	13
Kent	king, filter, hp	12	0.1	12
Pall Mall Light 100's	100mm, filter, menthol	12	1.1	12
Kent	king, filter	13	1.0	13
St. Moritz 100's	100mm, filter	14	1.1	13
Winston 100's	100mm, filter	14	1.0	14
Marlboro	king, filter, menthol	14	0.9	14
Eve Lights 120's	120mm, filter, menthol, hp	14	1.1	12
Alpine	king, filter, menthol	14	0.9	13
Eve Lights 120's	120mm, filter, hp	14	1.1	13
Salem	king, filter, menthol	14	1.1	14
Tareyton	king, filter	14	1.0	15
Tareyton 100's	100mm, filter	14	1.1	16
Kool Super Longs 100's	100mm, filter, menthol	14	1.0	16
Galaxy	king, filter	14	1.0	13
Kent 100's	100mm, filter	14	1.2	13
Montclair	king, filter, menthol	14	1.0	16
St. Moritz 100's	100mm, filter, menthol	14	1.1	14
Lark	king, filter	14	1.1	14
L & M	king, filter	14	1.1	14

Tar, Nicotine and Carbon Monoxide Content of Two Hundred (200)
Varieties of Domestic Cigarettes
(shown in increasing order of tar values)

BRAND	TYPE	TAR (mg/cig)	Nicotine (mg/cig)	Carbon Monoxide (mg/cig)
Marlboro	king, filter, menthol, hp	15	0.9	14
Viceroy	king, filter	15	1.0	16
Salem 100's	100mm, filter, menthol	15	1.1	14
Kent 100's	100mm, filter, menthol	15	1.2	14
L & M	king, filter, hp	15	1.0	14
Chesterfield	king, filter	15	1.0	15
Viceroy Super Longs 100's	100mm, filter	15	1.1	16
Saratoga 120's	120mm, filter, menthol, hp	15	1.0	16
Eve 100's	100mm, filter, menthol	15	1.2	14
L & M 100's	100mm, filter	15	1.1	16
Benson & Hedges	king, filter, hp	15	1.2	12
Oasis	king, filter, menthol	15	1.0	15
Eve 100's	100mm, filter	15	1.2	14
Saratoga 120's	102mm, filter, hp	15	1.0	16
Virginia Slims 100's	100mm, filter	15	1.0	15
Virginia Slims 100's	100mm, filter, menthol	15	1.0	14
Chesterfield 101	101mm, filter	15	1.1	16
DuMaurier	king, filter, hp	15	1.0	17
Raleigh	king, filter	15	1.0	17
Winston	king, filter	15	1.1	16
Long Johns 120's	120mm, filter, menthol	16	1.3	17
Raleigh 100's	100mm, filter	16	1.1	17
Kool	king, filter, menthol	16	1.1	17
Benson & Hedges 100's	100mm, filter, menthol, hp	16	1.0	15
Newport	king, filter, menthol, hp	16	1.2	16
Lark 100's	100mm, filter	16	1.2	15
Benson & Hedges 100's	100mm, filter, menthol	16	1.1	17
Camel	king, filter	16	1.2	16
Marlboro	king, filter, hp	16	1.0	14
Benson & Hedges 200's	100mm, filter, hp	16	1.1	16
Winston	king, filter, hp	16	1.1	15
Marlboro 100's	100mm, filter, hp	16	1.1	16
Philip Morris Internat'l 100's	100mm, filter, menthol, hp	16	1.0	15
Half & Half	king, filter	16	1.3	15
Marlboro 100's	100mm, filter	16	1.1	16
Kool	king, filter, menthol, hp	16	1.2	16
Tall 120's	120mm, filter, menthol	16	1.4	17
Benson & Hedges 100's	100mm, filter	16	1.1	16
Philip Morris Internat'l 100's	100mm, filter, hp	16	1.1	16
Marlboro	king, filter	16	1.0	15
Pall Mall 100's	100mm, filter	17	1.3	17
Old Gold Filters	king, filter	17	1.3	19
Tall 120's	120mm, filter	17	1.4	19
Newport	king, filter, menthol	17	1.3	18

Tar, Nicotine and Carbon Monoxide Content of Two Hundred (200) Varieties of Domestic Cigarettes
(shown in increasing order of tar values)

BRAND	TYPE	TAR (mg/cig)	Nicotine (mg/cig)	Carbon Monoxide (mg/cig)
Pall Mall	king, filter	18	1.2	18
Long Johns 120's	120mm, filter	18	1.4	18
Winston Internt'l 100's	100mm, filter	18	1.4	16
More 120's	120mm, filter	18	1.4	20
More 120's	120mm, filter, menthol	18	1.5	20
Max 120's	120mm, filter	19	1.6	18
Max 120's	120mm, filter, menthol	19	1.6	18
Spring 100's	100mm, filter, menthol	19	1.1	18
Kool	reg., non-filter, menthol	19	1.1	14
Picayune	reg., non-filter	19	1.4	15
Old Gold Filters	100mm, filter	20	1.5	20
Newport 100's	100mm, filter, menthol	10	1.6	20
Camel	reg., non-filter	21	1.4	13
Chesterfield	reg., non-filter	21	1.3	13
Philip Morris	reg., non-filter	21	1.4	12
Raleigh	king, non-filter	22	1.3	17
English Ovals	reg., non-filter, hp	23	1.7	12
Lucky Strike	reg., non-filter	24	1.5	17
Players	reg., non-filter, hp	24	1.9	14
Pall Mall	reg., non-filter	24	1.5	17
Chesterfield	king, non-filter	25	1.7	16
Old Gold Straight	king, non-filter	26	1.8	17
Philip Morris Commander	king, non-filter	27	1.7	15
Herbert Tareyton	king, non-filter	27	1.7	19
English Ovals	king, non-filter, hp	28	2.1	15
Bull Durham	king, filter	29	1.9	24

Source: Federal Trade Commission, December 1981.

1   TPM dry (tar)—milligrams total particulate matter less nicotine and water.
2   All results below 0.5 mg. "tar," 0.05 mg. nicotine and 0.5 mg. carbon monoxide reported as   0.5,   0.05,   0.5, respectively.
3   hp—hard pack

Appendix 2

Organizations and Services

American Cancer Society, 777 3rd Avenue, New York, New York, 10017.

American Health Foundation, 320 East 43rd St., New York, New York, 10017.

American Heart Association, 7320 Greenville Avenue, Dallas, Texas, 75231.

American Journal of Acupuncture, Inc., 1400 Lost Acre Drive, P.O. Box N-2, Felton, California, 95018.

American Lung Association, 1740 Broadway, New York, New York, 10019.

Biofeedback Society of America, 4301 Owens, Wheatridge, Colorado, 80303.

British Medical Association, BMA House, Tavistock Square, London, England WCIH 9JP.

Department of Health Education, Porter Memorial Hospital, 2525 South Downing, Denver, Colorado, 80210.

Federal Trade Commission, Office of Public Information, Pennsylvania Ave. and 6th St. N.W., Washington, D.C., 20580.

5-Day Plan To Stop Smoking, Seventh-Day Adventist Church, Narcotics Education Division, 6840 Eastern Avenue, N.W., Washington, D.C., 20012.

High Blood Pressure Information Center, 120/80 National Institute of Health, 710 Woodmont Ave. #1300, Bethseda, Maryland, 20214.

Narcotics Education, Inc., P.O. Box 4390, Washington, D.C., 20012.

National Interagency Council on Smoking and Health, 419 Park Avenue South, Suite 1301, New York, New York, 10016.

Office of Cancer Communications, National Cancer Institute, National Institutes of Health, Bethesda, Maryland, 20205.

Office on Smoking and Health, 158 Park Building, 5600 Fishers Lane, Rockville, Maryland, 20857.

St. Helena Hospital and Health Center, Deer Park, California, 94576.

Schick Centers, 2917 Fulton Avenue, Sacramento, California, 95821.

Shawnee Medical Center, 74th and Grandview, Shawnee Mission, Kansas, 66201.

SmokEnders, 50 Washington Street, Norwalk, Connecticut, 06854.

The Tobacco Institute, 1875 I Street N.W., Washington, D.C., 20006.

Bibliography

Books on the Dangers of Smoking

Die Tabaksucht und Ihre Bekaempfung, Prof. Dr. Paul Bernhard, 1965; Neuland Verlag Gesellschaft, Hamburg, West Germany.

The Health Consequences of Smoking: The Changing Cigarette, A Report of the Surgeon General, 1981; U.S. Dept. of Health and Human Services.

The Health Consequences of Smoking for Women. A Report of the Surgeon General, 1980; U.S. Dept. of Health and Human Services.

Books on How to Stop

Controlling the Smoking Epidemic, 1979; World Health Organization, Geneva, Switzerland.

How to Stop Smoking in 3 Days, Sidney Petrie, Florence Rhyn Serlin, Ph.D., 1973; Warner Books, New York, New York.

Kicking It: The New Way to Stop Smoking Permanently, Dr. David L. Geisinger, 1978; New American Library, Signet Books, New York, New York.

Kicking the Smoking Habit, by Boye De Mente, 1981; Phoenix Books, Phoenix, Arizona.

Lakewood's Stop Smoking Without Gaining Weight, Frank Hertle, 1978; Lakewood Publications, Inc.

Manual on Smoking Cessation Therapy, J. E. Brengelmann, 1978; Federal Centre for Health Education, Cologne, West Germany.

Nicht Mehr Rauchen, Meinrad Schaer, 1978; Blau Kreuz Verlag, Bern.

Smoking Programs for Youth, 1980; U.S. Dept. of Health and Human Services.

The Stop Smoking Book for Teens, Curtis Casewit, 1980; Messner, New York, New York.

Von Einem der Auszog, das Rauchen zu Lassen . . ., Helmut Rathert, 1979; Bastei Luebbe Publishing, West Germany.

Books on Health and Alternative Life Styles

Bibliography on Smoking and Health, World Health Organization, 1980; Informatics, Rockville, Maryland.

Directory of On-going Research in Smoking and Health, World Health Organization, Informatics, Rockville, Maryland.

Guide to Rational Living, Dr. A. Ellis, 1961; Englewood Ciffs, New Jersey.

Health for the Whole Person, A. C. Hastings Ph.D., J. Fadiman, Ph.D., James

S. Gordon M.D., 1981; Westview Press, Boulder, Colorado.

How to Use Your Mind to Heal Your Body, Norman Ford, 1980; Autumn Press, Brookline, Massachusetts.

Minding Your Body, Norman Ford, 1981; Autumn Press, Brookline, Massachusetts.

Take Charge of Your Health: the Complete Nutrition Book, Gladys Lindberg, 1982; Harper & Row, New York, New York.

The American Way of Life Need Not Be Hazardous to Your Health, John W. Farquhar, M.D., 1978; Stanford Alumni Association, Stanford, California.

The Best Doctors in the U.S., John Pekkanen, 1981; Seaview Books, New York, New York.

The Book of Health: A Complete Guide to Making Health Last a Lifetime, by The American Health Foundation, edited by Ernst L. Wynder, M.D., President, 1981; New York, New York.

The Cancer Syndrome, Ralph W. Moss, 1980; Grove, New York, New York.

The Well Body Book, Dr. Mike Samuels, 1973; Random House, New York, New York.

The Woman's Encyclopedia of Health and Natural Healing, Emrika Padus, 1981; Rodale Press, New York, New York.

Toward the Conquest of Cancer, Dr. E. J. Beattie, 1980; Crown, New York, New York.

Valley of the Sun Tape Instruction and Idea Manual, Dick Sutphen, 1981; Valley of the Sun Publishing, Malibu, California.

Other Books of Interest

Complete Meditation, Steve Kravette, 1981; Para Research, Rockport, Massachusetts.

Governing America, Joseph A. Califano, 1981; Simon & Schuster, New York, New York.

How to Hypnotize Yourself and Others, Rachel Copelan, 1981; Barnes and Noble Books, New York, New York.

Overcoming Procrastination, Albert Ellis and William Knaus, 1977; Institute for Rational Living, New York, New York.

Self-Mastery Through Self-Hypnosis, Dr. R. Bernhardt and David Martin, 1977; New American Library, Signet Books, New York, New York.

Staff Report on the Cigarette Advertising Investigation, James Sneed, 1981; Federal Trade Commission, U.S. Government Printing, Washington, D.C.

The Ladykillers, Why Smoking is a Feminist Issue, Bobbie Jacobsen, 1981; Continuum Books, New York, New York.

The Relaxation Response, Herbert Benson, 1975; William Morrow and Company, New York, New York.

Brochures, General Reports, Newsletters and Pamphlets

Dangers of Smoking—Benefits of Quitting, 1980; American Cancer Society, pamphlet, *I Quit Kit.*

Decade of Discovery: Advances in Cancer Research 1971-1981; National Cancer Institute, booklet.

Guide to Smoke-Free Dining, 1981; Group Against Smoking Pollution, pamphlet for different locations.

How to Choose a Stop Smoking Program, by Dr. Jerome L. Schwartz, Alan Rice, M.P.H., 1973; St. Helena Hospital and Health Center, booklet.

Life Lines Newsletter, P.O. Box 8551, Scottsdale, Arizona, 85252.

Me Quit Smoking? How/Why, 1980; American Lung Association, pamphlet.

Mind if I Smoke? 1979; Pacific Press, pamphlet.

Nurses: The Challenge to Action in Anti-Smoking Efforts, Judi Johnson, R.N., Ph.D., 1980; American Cancer Society, pamphlet.

Smoker's Self-Testing Kit, by Daniel Horn, Ph.D., 1980; U.S. Dept. of Health and Human Services, pamphlet.

Smoke Signals, 1981; Narcotics Education, Inc., newsletter.

Smoking and Health 1964-1979; The Continuing Controversy, 1979; The Tobacco Institute, booklet.

Smoking, Tobacco, and Health, a Fact Book; U.S. Dept. of Health and Human Services, booklet.

Strategic Withdrawal from Cigarette Smoking, by Arden G. Christen D.D.S. and Kenneth H. Cooper, M.D., 1979; American Cancer Society, report.

"Tar," Nicotine and Carbon Monoxide of the Smoke of 200 Varieties of Cigarettes, 1981; Federal Trade Commission, booklet.

The Present Status of the Five-Day Plans to Stop Smoking and an *In-patient Stop Smoking Plan* by Alan Rice, M.P.H., 1973; St. Helena Hospital and Health Center, booklet.

The Schick Story, 1980; Schick Centers, booklet.

Tobacco and Health, by John H. Holbrook, M.D., 1978; American Cancer Society, booklet.

You Can Kick the Habit! by Walter Kloss, 1976; the 5-Day Plan, Portland Adventist Medical Center, booklet.

Index